The Films of
MAMIE VAN DOREN

The Films of
Mamie Van Doren

by Joseph Fusco

BearManor Media
2010

The Films of Mamie Van Doren
© 2010 Joseph Fusco

All rights reserved.

For information, address:

BearManor Media
P. O. Box 71426
Albany, GA 31708

bearmanormedia.com

Cover design by John Teehan

Typesetting and layout by John Teehan

Published in the USA by BearManor Media

ISBN—1-59393-532-3

Table of Contents

Introduction: A Montage of Inamoratas 1

The Films of Mamie Van Doren

Jet Pilot (1949) - released: 1957 51
Two Tickets to Broadway (1951) 55
Footlight Varieties (1951) 59
His Kind of Woman (1951) 63
Forbidden (1953) 67
The All American (1953) 71
Hawaiian Nights (1954) 77
Yankee Pasha (1954) 79
Francis Joins the WACs (1954) 85
The Second Greatest Sex (1955) 91
Ain't Misbehavin' (1955) 97
Running Wild (1955) 103
Star in the Dust (1956) 109
The Girl In Black Stockings (1957) 115
Untamed Youth (1957) 121
La Bellissime gambe di Sabrina (1958) 127
Teacher's Pet (1958) 131
High School Confidential (1958) 135
Born Reckless (1958) 143
Guns, Girls and Gangsters (1959) 149

The Beat Generation (1959)	155
The Big Operator (1959)	161
Girls Town (1959)	167
Vice Raid (1959)	175
Sex Kittens Go to College (1960)	181
The Private Lives of Adam and Eve (1961)	187
College Confidential (1960)	193
The Blonde from Buenos Aires (1961)	199
The Candidate (1964)	201
3 Nuts in Search of a Bolt (1964)	207
The Sheriff Was a Lady (1964)	213
The Las Vegas Hillbillys (1966)	219
The Navy vs. the Night Monsters (1966)	225
You've Got To Be Smart (1967)	229
Voyage To the Planet of Prehistoric Women (1968)	233
The Arizona Kid (1971)	237
Free Ride (1986)	241
Glory Years (TVM) (1987)	245
The Vegas Connection (TVM) (1999)	249
Slackers (2002)	251

Appendices

I. Television Credits	255
II. Theater	259
III. Discography	261
IV. Books	263

Introduction: A Montage of Inamoratas

American pop culture has garnered many myths involving archetypes, prototypes, and stereotypes. A category of eternal romance was the myth of the Vamp, a power icon that wielded an influence that defied the boundaries of servitude. She possessed the power to lure the soul out of a man's body and kill him with leftover regrets. Through a tragic and extreme scenario, the Vamp nurtured her suitor and inspired him to develop his innate talents to achieve forbidden dreams. Only one partner survived the fatal attraction when that happened.

Traditionally, the Vamp was a dark-haired beauty, the femme-fatale who was the conquered man's excuse to justify his shortcomings. The Vamp's payback was often public disgrace, social ostracism or ignoble death. It was rarely a guilt-free happy ending.

The heir to Adam's folly was being the child of two wives whose idea of power sex was being the first Succubus in Eden. She has lived everywhere—from Sumer to Victorian England—and has been celebrated and railed against in every culture's art, music, theater and mythology.

During the 20th Century, the silver screen became the means of expressing and defining some of the Vamp's power schemes. The major change was the complexion of the lady conqueror: the dark hues of the silent years turned to gold with the use of sound. It was also the start of a Depression that shared its birth pangs with the arrival of a new Vamp - the Blonde Bombshell.

The three ages of the Blonde Bombshell were the '30s Depression-Era Beauty, the '40s Wartime Pin-up Phase and the '50s Dynasty of Platinum Blondes. Each age had a reigning queen and a sub-stratum of royalty and they followed a ritual that included public adulation and private sacrifices. Sometimes, the idolatry turned into tragedy and the adulation into mourning.

Jean Harlow was the seminal blonde femme-fatale, the one who created the world of the tragic celluloid goddess. 1933, George Hurrell.

During the '30s, Jean Harlow provided dreams for the Depression years. She was the seminal platinum goddess, the founder of the cult of peroxide blondes. Harlow was responsible for reversing the brunette Vamp into an ambitious blonde, previously the bright good-girl type. She made 36 films in a decade's reign. Notable films included *Hell's Angel, The Public Enemy, Platinum Blonde, Dinner at Eight, Bombshell* and *Saratoga*.

Harlow's life also set the dye for the dark sides of the blonde bombshell mythology. Her husband, MGM producer Paul Bern, committed suicide at her home and the mysterious circumstances created one of Hollywood's first lurid tabloid scandals. An extramarital affair with Max Baer, the Heavyweight Champion, did not help to smooth things over. Her death at the age of 26 from kidney failure enshrined her platinum locks, deep-set eyes, cleft chin and painted eyebrows forever in Hollywood historiography.

Harlow's cuddly silkiness had its opposite in the brassy dominance of Mae West. She had written and starred in Broadway plays before making films in Hollywood and she had a patented bawdy style that no one else could copy. If anyone is the embodiment of the positive power of a blonde bombshell in real life, it was Mae West.

Meaty, delicious, boisterous and bold, she was a multi-faceted woman who went beyond the two-dimensional image of the vapid tease queen. She was also creative, intelligent and fiercely independent. Living in a world run by men was no problem for Mae West because she had the power to run men with little or no effort.

The censors were her biggest obstacle, but she always found a way around them to express herself. Themes like sexual liberation, female independence and gay rights were championed by Mae West a half a century before they could be discussed in public.

The titles to some of her films say it all about the brassy survivor: *I'm No Angel, She Done Him Wrong, Klondike Annie, Belle of the Nineties* and *My Little Chickadee*.

It was no different with the era that eclipsed the Depression. The wartime spirit was aflame during the '40s when one bad dream ended and another one started. Golden ladies and dark sunshine girls produced a variety of blondes suitable to comedy, light drama and crime *noirs*. They had different faces and touched different emotions but they led to the same end: male servitude. They were credible alternatives to each other and they held sway over the cheap imitations and flash-in-the pans.

Pinups of the girl next door steamed and shriveled from the fiery temptations of Veronica Lake and Lana Turner. Lake and Turner have star-crossed biographies with twists of fortune that led to vistas and dead ends. Veronica Lake was not very lucky and she would experience a descent into madness after her popularity waned to the vanishing point. Her captivating style was enhanced by a stream of hair that flowed around her right eye. It was the mystery touch and kept her going through classic comedies, dramas and fantasies.

Lake starred in *Sullivan's Travels* ('41) and *So Proudly We Hail!* ('43), two wartime morale boosters. *This Gun For Hire* ('42) and *The Blue Dahlia* ('46) are crime *noirs*. *I Married a Witch* ('42) and *Out of This World* ('45) are dark fantasies made at the beginning and the end of World War II. Her life changed for the worse when her Hollywood star burned out; she hit the skids and suffered from acute paranoia.

Lana Turner's smoldering attitude and smooth style cast the mold for the new post-war made-to-order streamlined blonde. It was a manner that made *The Postman Always Rings Twice* ('46) and *Cass Timberlane* ('47) forbidden delights. She also enflamed Robert Louis Stevenson's madman with the split personality in the period piece shocker *Dr. Jekyll and Mr. Hyde* ('41).

Lana Turner was one of a handful of sex symbols who weathered the mishaps and scandals to hold her ground in the '50s with *The Bad and the Beautiful* ('52), *Flame and the Flesh* ('54) *Peyton Place* ('57) and *Imitation of Life* ('59). She made periodic returns, once in *Madame X* ('66) and on television's *Falcon Crest* ('82-'83).

The postwar era was the nuclear age and its queen was Marilyn Monroe. She was a personified contradiction: cheap and accessible while being refined and remote. Class and crass were contrasts defined by her slaves of the moment. Men were driven insane by her charms, a power so strong that it created the need for replicas to satisfy the slave population's desire.

Gentlemen Prefer Blondes ('53), *How to Marry a Millionaire* ('53), *The Seven Year Itch* ('55), *Bus Stop* ('56) and *Some Like It Hot* ('59) were textbooks on how to be the conquering blonde or the number one enslaved harem stooge. During the '50s, the myth of the Blonde became public policy via Madison Avenue's coronation campaigns.

The best medium to display the myth was the one that created Marilyn Monroe: the movies. American males soon satisfied their re-

Introduction: A Montage of Inamoratas 5

Mae West was a self-made power fetish with strength, intelligence and bodacious beauty. 1933, Paramount.

Veronica Lake added a dark mystique to the crime femme-fatale. 1940, Robert Riche for Paramount.

pressed instincts with genuine articles, dime store imitations and better-than-nothings.

In the '50s, the parade of others included Sheree North, Joi Lansing, Cleo Moore, Barbara Nichols, Leigh Snowden and dozens more. Of the parade of others, only Jayne Mansfield became Marilyn Monroe's familial twin. Mansfield was larger than life, a cartoon caricature of the Blonde Goddess. She played it stupid and top-heavy, an exaggerated persona that was a direct consequence of competing with the scores of Marilyn progeny to the nth degree.

Although she appeared in more than twenty-five movies from 1954 to 1968, Mansfield is noted primarily for two movies, *The Girl Can't Help It* ('56) and *Will Success Spoil Rock Hunter?* ('57). Lost among the tinsel and glamour are the obscure gems: *Illegal* ('55), a courtroom procedural with Edward G. Robinson, *The Burglar* ('57), an offbeat crime drama starring Dan Duryea, and the electrifying *The George Raft Story* ('61) with Ray Danton.

Marilyn Monroe and Jayne Mansfield represented the extremities of the '50s Blonde Power Fetish, displaying a range that started with vixen cunning and ended with poodle tricks and bad jokes. Their common descent into Hell was the official kiss of death for the cult and occurred at the beginning and the end of the Sixties. It was the decade that de-glamorized blonde bombshells as reigning prom queens and sent them into the jungles of the new world.

As is the case with extremes, there is a third point that creates a balance. In the myth of the '50s Blonde Bombshell, Mamie Van Doren provides the ballast. She did not enjoy the mass appeal of Marilyn Monroe nor was she the honky-tonk sideshow that was Jayne Mansfield. Harsh critics considered her a pretender to the throne; at most, they called her Queen of the B's.

Mamie has experienced the Hollywood constellation, tabloid scrutiny routine, nightclub paradise circuit and jungle hells of the '60s rebellion as an actress, pinup queen, nightclub entertainer and war zone entertainer. In Mamie's World, harem girls mix it up with Venusian Amazons, the power of rock 'n' roll belongs to women, female conquerors never take no for an answer and Salome sings while doing her dance of the seven veils. For them, a head on a silver platter is merely an appetizer.

Double entendres, suggestive poses and sensual song-and-dance numbers comprised a potent sensuality for Mamie Van Doren's films. Independence and the ability to outdo male schemers was also a part of the heated mix. This defiant attitude of rebellion and independence marked the characters that typified her best work. They were women who meted out paydays that inspired blue-collar Joes to reach for the brass ring, only to wish they were never born.

Most blonde bombshells found a persona and stuck with it throughout their careers, but Mamie Van Doren displayed the different faces and personalities that went with the platinum hair and the bullet bras. There were identities beyond the postwar years, each portraying a fair shaded tease that added seasoning to the original. The variety of Mamie Van Doren's roles proves that her star was not cut out of a cookie-cutter mold.

Van Doren's characters constantly crossed the borders that separated the different states of blonde bondage. There were airheads with nerves of steel, streetwise dames who lost their bites when they went soft inside because of love, older women whose passion was fresher than young panther girls on the prowl and homecoming queens who grew up to be mature losers.

The one thing that unites these women is the stage that they strut their stuff on is a world of power run by men. The choicest of Mamie's characters defy this system; some of them are destroyed by this setup but others are the destroyers. The power of these women is so strong that even the losers take down their opponents in their defeat.

The gold diggers have the power to change a man's destiny into a tawdry pleasure. They are naïve glamour girls trying to snare a rich husband, obvious in their intent and unabashed in going after what they want. Wide-eyed giggly types, they see the value of a man in the fatness of his assets, holdings and swine ethics. Susie Ward, Jackie, Harriet Ames and Peggy DeFore are card-carrying members of the Platinum Club.

In *The All American*, Susie Ward is a waitress working in a dive where wayward Ivy League college students become hooks for marriage and a better life. Susie Ward may play it dumb and flattering for the sugar daddies at the college parties, but the wheels are turning and she can help and hurt with equal ease. She is the heroine at the end of the film, someone who earns the respect of the bluebloods who carry her off on their shoulders for a final victory toss.

Jackie is a chorus girl who makes old society men feel young again in *Ain't Misbehavin'*. She coos and dances but when an old scion's fingerprints become cheeky she pitches the garden path for a well-lit dance floor. Jackie is spun from gold and desires more of the same to make her shine. It has a ring that makes her giddy.

Harriet Ames is the kiss-off to the curvaceous airhead who blew more hot air than a heated bellows in *The Girl in Black Stockings*. She is the companion of a washed-up actor who seeks rejuvenation at a Utah

Introduction: A Montage of Inamoratas   9

Lana Turner stripped off the blinders and melt her competition with her head-on delivery. 1946, Metro-Goldwyn-Meyer.

vacation spot. Grisly murders are the backdrop to the May-December fan club. The act becomes a single when the fan club loses its only groupie.

Peggy DeFore is a nightclub singer who keeps it real for the King, Clark Gable, in *Teacher's Pet*. She sings "The Girl Who Invented Rock

Marilyn Monroe reinvented the blonde bombshell craze in the 50's with an image made from an original vision. 1953, Frank Powolny.

and Roll" to Gable before turning to the blues when Doris Day enters the picture. Mid-western blonde versus urban sunshine is the tug of war that stretches the old king.

For the hot rod streamers, rock 'n' roll is the breakdown music. Irma Bean, Penny Lowe and Silver Morgan are quintessential '50s hot rod girls. Bean is a jitterbugging teen having good times with a member of a car-jacking outfit in *Running Wild*. Lowe and her sister are entertainers hitchhiking their way to stardom in *Untamed Youth*. In *Girls Town*, Silver Morgan is a heads-up toss between the rival hot rod gangs.

Some of the dark clouds that follow bad luck hot rod girls are oppressive authority figures and reformatories where rules and regulations mean nothing to them. Irma Bean's last dance is a dead-end shootout for her boyfriend; Penny Lowe does bumps and grinds on a cotton plantation; and Silver Morgan defends herself against the rules of a Catholic home for wayward girls.

Not every sprightly blonde found an ideal man and started the perfect family. For every blonde who gets the brass ring there were dozens that floated off into life's black holes. They are the twilight bombshells, lost souls who share a fate that is cashed in without redemption.

Carol Hudson of *Vice Raid* and Vi Victor of *Guns, Girls and Gangsters* play high stakes power games in worlds run by men. They are lucky charms that turn deadly for their mascot employers. Irony is what they reap: for Victor, it's a mockery of her name and for Hudson it's a clean slate back to the small-town life.

Saxie Symbol and Samantha Ashley are the end of the line for bump-and-grind chorus girl bombshells. In *3 Nuts in Search of a Bolt* and *The Candidate*, media manipulation and shady politics are the last sugar daddies left at the party.

The seven women are worlds apart yet are connected by their need to overcome threats and obstacles to their sovereignty. They are independent thinkers whose sexuality is a form of empowerment, not a false identity forced upon them by twisted male ideals. They accept their challenges and turn them into a final triumph, leaving pieces of the power structure in their victory wake.

Many of Mamie's minor characters are also worlds apart yet share a common bond. Jackie, the chorus girl in 1955's *Ain't Misbehavin'* could easily be the fresh face of Mrs. Van Graaf in 2002's *Slackers*. The stop in between is Saxie Symbol in *3 Nuts in Search of a Bolt*, made in 1964.

Symbol is the chorus girl-turned-cynical stripper without a clue in the world about longshoremen or grappling hooks because psychiatry is her alibi. The half-century showbiz road is a final pass through the theater's back door exit and the trap door booby prize is becoming a broken-down dock queen laid up in the hospital.

Nurses have held a special place as fantasy figures, but Nora and Nurse Stratton are two different nurses in vastly different circumstances. *The Navy vs. the Night Monsters* and *Free Ride* may deal with omnivorous appetites, but one is a hell and the other is a heaven. It is a matter of hungry mobile trees on a Pacific atoll or horny college students in a '80s campus comedy. Both movies are separated by twenty years.

Harems and clans have a social order that separate the weak from the strong. There are leaders and followers; those who give the orders and the others that obey. It is a pecking order where defiance breaks subservience and the reward is leadership of the clan.

Lilith, the harem girl in *Yankee Pasha*, is a polar twin of Moana, the queen of the sea clan in *Voyage to the Planet of Prehistoric Women*. The worlds of the two women are opposites: Morocco is opulent and ruled by iron manhood and Venus is the water sign that gives women wings to ride the waves.

The western Mamie is a collection of characters that are like different lunar phases. In *Star in the Dust* ('56), Ellen Ballard shoots with conviction and changes her inheritance by taking a stand. She cuts the family ties and blindfolds her blood kin in a final showdown. *The Arizona Kid* ('71) is a Filipino western where Sharon Miller is more svelte and felicitous than Ballard, but shoots to survive an Indian attack and speaks with a dubbed tongue. She has the shapely shape in a bustier that inspires a nerd to impersonate a notorious gunslinger in a showdown with a deadly outlaw.

Jackie Adams is the rodeo queen and nightclub performer who ropes the steers in *Born Reckless*. She is as sharp riding as she is singing and has a good time showing it in trick riding and hearty songs. Ten years later, Boots Malone is belting out songs and serving beer to patrons in a broken-down honky-tonk in the drive-in specialty *The Las Vegas Hillbillys*. She is a saloon spirit, there for guiding the new owner but ready to disappear into thin air when her contract is up.

Birdie Sneider's love laments about the single parson are expressed in song and dance in *The Second Greatest Sex* ('55), but Olivia, the dance hall queen of a different kind, sings her heart out for the man who owns everything in West Germany's *The Sheriff Was a Lady* ('64). Birdie and Olivia are two faces at the other end of the music scale yet sing the same song in different tempos.

Mamie had the added dimensions of being a pin-up queen and a part of the vanguard of rock 'n' roll in Hollywood films. These two additional

Introduction: A Montage of Inamoratas 13

Jayne Mansfield became a tragic parody of the blonde femme-fatale mythology. 1956, 20th. Century Fox.

factors were enough to raise the collective temperature of the Legion of Decency and it consistently refused to give her movies a stamp of approval.

Pin-up magazines of the Fifties dealt with the strict moral code by exploiting voluptuous curves and seductive smiles with faux labia painted lips. Forbidden sex was thinly masked by a girlish smile or an innocent facial expression.

Skimpy dresses, low-cut gowns, bathing suits or a baggy men's shirt were some of the ways that helped define sexy shapes. Bending over, curling in a chair or reclining on the beach were the poses that were meant to unnerve voyeuristic spectators. It was a case of image more than substance and a matter of fantasy over reality, all for the sake of satisfying the male libido by performing the ritual dance of the phallus.

This was the norm during the Fifties, when big bosoms and well-rounded bottoms were the male obsession, as evidenced by the revolutionary impact of Hugh Hefner's *Playboy* magazine, which debuted in 1954. It is no small wonder that the first Playmate was Marilyn Monroe, the quintessential Fifties Blonde Bombshell.

Mamie Van Doren's steamy image and silky elegance was magnified in popular pin-ups and pocket magazines. She was a Vargas Girl in *Esquire* magazine in 1951. Her photos and glossies have appeared in '50s pocket magazines like *Vue*, *Tempo* and *Modern Man* and fanzines such as *Picturegoer* and *Photoplay*. In 1964, she appeared in *Playboy* to publicize *3 Nuts in Search of a Bolt*. Her portfolio includes studio publicity stills, popular magazine spreads, bathing suit teases and nude studies.

Print exposure in the gossip columns mixed with the glamour of the pin-ups to form a public opinion about the screen image. Love affairs, nightclub appearances and peccadilloes all provided grist for the mill. If sexpot was the category than the stories that filled the columns had to give the public what they expected. That included the fans and the foes; sometimes, that meant both.

Mamie Van Doren's detractors were as diverse as Cardinal Spellman and Louella Parsons; both could attack from different angles. It was understandable - she was the vapid glamour girl who gave it up to become the hard luck knucklebuster whose sexuality was an added will to power. She was condemned for living on the other side of the tracks, the same place where religious hypocrites and self-righteous gossip scribes let it all hang out when they turned their collars around or hid behind the columns to do their things.

During the Fifties, the bad girl attitude was condemned by public decency but secretly relished by a hypocritical society. It was a time when every norm had its own taboo. When rhythm and blues splintered into rock 'n' roll, the up-tempo attitude with a backbeat became an electric tidal wave that only rebels surfed.

Mamie Van Doren synthesized the traits of her predecessors and became an American original. 1955, Universal Pictures Company, Inc.

Some purists maintain that rock 'n' roll was created by the first barrelhouse piano player who plied his craft as an accompanist in a turn-of-the century New Orleans bordello. Anonymous he may remain, but the left-handed riff that he created started a revolution nearly a half a century later.

Royal titles of kings and queens and large claims of creators and absconders may obscure the beauty of the music, but it all springs from one thing and that's what was happening in the turn-of-the century cathouses. Boogie Woogie and rock 'n' roll meant the same thing and the symbol that represented it was someone who embodied that attitude.

Marilyn Monroe was an icon of the Fifties even though she was never associated with the music that was one of the hallmarks of the decade. Her big song-and-dance number is "Diamonds are a Girl's Best Friend" from *Gentlemen Prefer Blondes*. It defined the personality that was a lure for sugar daddies, sophisticated gentlemen and sad sacks.

Jayne Mansfield starred in the rock 'n' roll classic, *The Girl Can't Help It*, but did not step out of her sexpot character. She was the fulfillment of the working man's fantasy and was incidental to the movie's musical theme. It was the appearance of many of the era's great rock 'n' rollers that gave the film authenticity.

Mamie's first rock 'n' roll movie was *Running Wild*. In it, Bill Haley and his Comets performed "Razzle-Dazzle" on the jukebox, but it was the stripped down big band arrangements that really made *Running Wild* a rock 'n' roll movie. Irma Bean performs her jitterbug to a streamlined swing tune yet it is rock 'n' roll!

Untamed Youth was Mamie's second rock 'n' roll movie and it was a brutal plantation melodrama. Mamie sang four songs and performed some hot dance numbers in the barracks and on a television set banana boat. Eddie Cochran sang a song in the cotton fields, too. The real rock 'n' roll was the big band tunes that drove the teen inmates crazy at Pinky's mess hall.

The Platters sing a song in *Girls Town*. Mamie serenades Clark Gable with her signature song, "The Girl Who Invented Rock and Roll" in *Teacher's Pet*. Rockabilly is the style of *Born Reckless*.

Van Doren's movies with Albert Zugsmith had constant references to the music, including appearances by innovators or derivatives. Louis Armstrong and his All Stars perform a couple of New Orleans-flavored jazz songs in *The Beat Generation*. In the same movie, Ray Danton recites a beat poem about rockets to the moon. Vampira recites a poem about tomorrow being nowhere in *High School Confidential*. Jackie Coogan's house band backs her up with Dixieland riffs. Jerry Lee Lewis opens the movie with a performance on the flatbed of a truck.

Mamie Van Doren could also shake up the dance floor. The '50s mindset was prone to her type of arousal. It's all there in her musical numbers!

Penny Lowe's barracks dance in *Untamed Youth* illustrates why a silk stocking and a bare leg are lethal weapons; this, in spite of a campy rock 'n' roll song about infidelity called "Salamander." Penny shakes, rattles and rolls for her fellow inmates while her sister strums a guitar and adds the rhythm.

A peeper is blinded by a butch's octopus moment. His buddies laugh as he pays the price for spying on the ritual dance. The corny song is enough for Penny to rasp with an attitude that chops away at weak knees. Blame it all on the invention of silk stockings.

Vi Victor's fluorescent congas in *Guns, Girls and Gangsters* are spiced with Latin rhythms. "Anything Your Heart Desires" is a Las Vegas type of mating call revue. A big band and a male chorus are the ceremonial props to Mamie. She is like a queen of the jungle as she glitters and shakes in two time zones. Her chorus boys are human settees who serve their mistress well.

The color grind of bumps and tassels in *3 Nuts in Search of a Bolt* is Mamie's salute to the lost art of the striptease. She performs it the way it was meant to be, as a slow torment of expecting to see something that you were never going to see. Saxie Symbol is the burlesque queen at the end of an era that started at the turn of the century.

Add to this the brief dance Carol Hudson does for Whitey Brandon in the hotel set-up in *Vice Raid*. Hudson wears a white bathing suit and matching heels as she wiggles across the floor. Ironically, he is the one who is suspended after he busts her.

There is a dream sequence in the unedited version of *Sex Kittens Go to College,* where several stripteasers take it all off in an R-rated way for a comatose Thinko the Robot. The dances are meant to revive the humanoid computer, the victim of a nervous breakdown. Later, Mamie performs a series of wild dances at the Passion Pit with a Texas oil man, a public relations man and three oversexed middle-aged college professors. Her function at the junction is a sequence of sensual dance styles that surpasses the combined impact of the strippers. She is the reason Thinko blew his microchip.

Mamie Van Doren was a question of opposites from the start: a child of the dust bowl who would become a glamorous movie star and a farmer's daughter who was anything but the stereotype in the traveling salesman's joke book.

Warner and Lucille Olander became parents to a daughter on February 6, 1933, in Rowena, South Dakota. Her mother named the girl Joan, after Joan Crawford. It was the first connection with Hollywood, the

18   The Films of Mamie Van Doren

Mamie Van Doren made her debut at Universal-International as a smoky voiced nightclub singer in *Forbidden*. 1953, Universal Pictures Company, Inc.

second being born into the atypical small Depression-era immigrant town, a seedbed for celluloid dreams and careers on the silver screen.

Rowena was settled by German, Swedish, Norwegian and Irish immigrants. It was the rich bloodline of her Swedish heritage and the work ethic of her Depression-era family that instilled an iron clad will to challenge and overcome unfavorable odds.

For Joan, the change from rural to urban came when her family moved to Sioux City, Iowa, in 1939. One of her new experiences included seeing her first motion picture. During the Depression, movies were a way out of the misery of having nothing and facing the prospects of a desolate future. The ticket holders could one day live the glamorous lives of their favorite stars; it was a matter of dreaming the dream that was on the screen. The reigning queen of the time was Jean Harlow and she inspired Joan Olander to become a movie star.

The Olander family moved to Hollywood in 1942. Mother and daughter shared a love for movies and would read fanzines and attend movie premieres. Joan acquired her first autograph at a premiere and it was from Mae West. Working in movie theatres was also a way for starstruck teenagers to satisfy their screen romances. In 1946, she became an usherette at the Pantages Theater, the famous art-deco movie palace in Hollywood. For aspiring starlets, the path to stardom also included modeling and beauty contests. Each job was a step closer to the Hollywood contract.

Niles Thorn Granlund (NTG) was a part of the nascent television industry. He had a fifteen-minute show where he hawked products showcased by young models. They were accompanied by flower girls. Joanie, the Little Flower Girl on NTG's television show, was the next step to the dream factory. That was followed by a stint as a singer with Ted Fio Rito's orchestra. The beauty contests paid off in 1948 with titles for Miss Eight Ball and Miss Palm Springs. The titles gave her exposure through publicity and public appearances. She met people in the business and caught the eye of admirers. One of the admirers was Howard Hughes.

Assistants and lackeys conducted phone interviews and gave instructions on how to dress for the luncheon meeting with the boss. The aspiring starlet used the tips and avoided the boss's maneuvers, but landed a contract with RKO. The studio's movies were peons to the glory days of the '40s, encompassing crowd-pleasing genres like war pictures, crime dramas, romantic musicals and the variety revue format.

Joan Olander had bit parts in four RKO films produced by Howard Hughes: *Jet Pilot* ('49), *His Kind of Woman* ('51), *Two Tickets to Broadway* ('51), and *Footlight Varieties* ('51). She may have been an unbilled extra, but she appeared in movies that starred John Wayne, Janet Leigh, Robert Mitchum and Jane Russell. Howard Hughes produced them and two were directed by D.W. Griffith and Josef von Sternberg.

A successful movie career with RKO seemed unlikely so a change in plans was in order. Joan Olander migrated to New York, where she danced as a showgirl and appeared in musicals, chief being Monte Proser's *Billion Dollar Baby,* starring Jackie Gleason. Jimmy McHugh, a popular songwriter, used her in his musicals and became her manager. He arranged for a screen test at 20th Century-Fox, which was looking for a Betty Grable type. The actress with the winning screen test was Marilyn Monroe. Other screen tests at MGM, Paramount and Columbia were unsuccessful because of her resemblance to Monroe.

McHugh's companion was Louella Parsons, the powerful gossip columnist. She was not fond of the business relationship between McHugh and Olander and used her considerable influence to make things hard for the aspiring actress. Parsons was not powerful enough to derail her ambition, however, and the Hollywood contract came from Universal-International when one of its agents, Phil Benjamin, saw Olander as Marie, the young girl, in a stage performance of *Come Back, Little Sheba*, directed by Aaron Spelling.

It was a contract with Universal-International Studios that started a new phase of her career. The moment Joan Olander was christened Mamie Van Doren, she became part of the platinum blonde pantheon that dominated Hollywood in the '50s.

Universal Studios was founded in 1912 by Carl Laemmle. He created a dream factory that would continue without him and adapt to the changes of the subsequent decades to enjoy renewed success after successive slumps. The silent years and the golden age of horror were followed by doldrums that were cured by a new horror wave and the Deanna Durbin years. Their popularity spelled success for the studio, but ran the course in the postwar period. The solution to the new doldrums was a merger with International Studios in 1946.

The revolving globe remained, but standards were modified to fit the demands of the changing movie market. A variety of genres would provide the goods for double features and they would star the kings and

Jackie lays it on thick for a prospective sugar daddy (Reginald Gardinier) in *Ain't Misbehavin'*. 1955, Universal Pictures Company, Inc.

queens of previous eras, along with the young actors and actresses groomed by the studio to become the new generation of stars.

Each year a spate of up-and-comers received the star treatment, including public relations send-offs to acquaint the public with U-I's new faces. The studio signed Mamie Van Doren in 1953 and launched her as a rival to Marilyn Monroe with her medium-blonde coif, caring eyes, blood-red lips and well-rounded hips.

The print medium reinforced the sexpot persona, sometimes at the behest of a successful press agent or manager while often relying on imagination and innuendo. Fan magazines and gossip columns were the best venues to keep the rising stars in the public eye. *Screenland, Photo, Gala* and *Celebrity* magazines were instrumental in making the Marilyn connection early in Mamie Van Doren's career. *Cine Revue, Silver Screen, Movie Stars* and *Movieland Pin-Ups* were magazines devoted to highlighting plot synopses and showcasing the latest photos of stars at gala premieres or out on the town.

Just call me MAMIE!

With breathtaking proportions, silver blonde hair and teasing brown eyes, Mamie Van Doren is the likeliest challenge to Marilyn Monroe

By Tom Carlson

A SILVER-BLONDE dynamo known as Mamie Van Doren is stirring up more electricity at Universal-International than all the studio generators put together. She's the biggest threat to Marilyn Monroe that any studio has been able to find so far. And they've all been looking hard! In the short space of eight hours, an unknown singer named Joan Olander emerged from obscurity to become the most talked-about girl on the U-I lot. Producer Ted Richmond, looking for a sultry brunette for a one-day bit part in "Forbidden," saw Joan, changed the role to a blonde, and Joan to Mamie Van Doren. Mamie's new name, is, of course, a tribute to the popularity of our new First Lady. The Hollywood Mamie, who's created all the "stop-Monroe" furor, stands 5'4", and weighs 112 pounds, breathtakingly distributed over a 36-bust, 24-waist, 35-hips figure. Born in Rowena, S. D., she's lived in Los Angeles since she was eight. Made her professional debut as vocalist with Ted Flo Rita's orchestra at a Las Vegas supper club. There (CONTINUED ON PAGE 56)

Queen at 20th, Marilyn may find popularity threatened.

In just one day Mamie emerged from obscurity and stirred up a tremendous furor.

Mamie Van Doren is launched as the likeliest challenge to Marilyn Monroe. June 1953, Screenland.

The June issue of *Screenland* magazine heralded the arrival of Mamie Van Doren with the headline, "Just Call Me Mamie" and declared her a candidate to challenge Marilyn. "Mamie Moves in on Marilyn" is the headline for *Photo* in 1953 and a blurb announced, "Blonde, brash and bound for stardom...she is the dynamic new Monroe threat." It is typical of her public relations buildup. Pretty soon, she was being featured in fanzines likes *Tempo, Photo, Gala, Look, Cine Revue, Silver Screen, Celebrity, Picturegoer, Photoplay* and *Tempo/Quick.*

It took a strenuous training regimen to back up the public relations boast. 6:00 A.M. wake calls led to dance classes an hour later. Rehearsals, publicity photo sessions were scheduled along with diction, acting classes and horseback riding and fencing lessons. The added requirements were film premieres, publicity junkets and media interviews.

Hollywood's newest Monroe threat had the vital statistics that balanced a light I.Q., something that was germane to the upwardly mobile blonde hussy. Mamie Van Doren's parts at U-I were mainly man-hungry gold diggers. That aspect was also standard fare in the manual on how to marry a millionaire. Dim bulbs and hungry for riches was a long line of fair-skinned and golden-trellised tease queens, the exception being her last role for the studio in an offbeat Western.

Her career at U-I offered movies that ran the full spectrum of the studio's diverse popular genres: a black-and-white suspense crime drama, a musical short, a class-conscious football movie, a CinemaScope Arabian Nights adventure, a comic novelty that was losing its novelty, color musicals in the Old West and on the '50s West Coast and a bizarre Western revenge tale.

Van Doren's first role for the studio was a cameo that relied heavily on sensual allure. She played a sultry nightclub chanteuse in *Forbidden* and sang a burning rendition of "You Belong to Me," the theme song of Tony Curtis' star-crossed-love adventure.

After the cameo, she had her first large part in *The All American,* another Tony Curtis film. She plays Susie Ward, a waitress in a bar that is off-limits to the jocks at the local college. Football is the reason the college exists and being an All American is a shining beacon for an heir to old money.

Susie Ward is Mamie's first substantial part. It is a supporting role and she is billed third in the credits. She has a routine of entrapment for any of the students that stray from the hallowed halls of ivy. Every wayward college student becomes a hook for marriage. She has a personality to match the body, using non-sequiturs and an innocent charm to hide a manipulative mind, something that is consistent with most of Mamie Van Doren's roles at U-I.

The All American was followed by another cameo as a tropical tease in *Hawaiian Nights,* a short comedy highlighted by Pinky Lee's one-liners and hula dancers.

The studio had a well-rounded roster of genres that were audience pleasers. Costume Sagas still lived on the studio's lot and that could mean anything from a Technicolor Arabian adventure or a compelling *High Noon* clone. They were impressive, in a kid's storybook sort of way.

Other popular items were the seasoned series that paid the studio bills. They were slapstick-based comedies that chronicled the comedic exploits of Ma and Pa Kettle, Abbott and Costello and Francis the Talking Mule.

Mamie Van Doren had roles in *Yankee Pasha* and *Francis Joins the WACS*, both made in 1954. Lilith and Corporal Bunky Hilstrom are members of exclusive clubs for women: a Middle Eastern harem and the WACS.

Mamie tested against Mari Blanchard and Lisa Gaye for the role of Lilith. She got the part and they wound up in the harem. Lilith is a storybook concubine, prized because of her fairness and willingness to please. She is a chatterbox and that leads to comic exchanges. The challenge that defines her is the climax of the film where she helps to betray the Omar Id-Din and survive the plot to help the hero reclaim his New World woman.

Francis Joins the WACS is the fifth film in the popular series. Mamie plays Corporal Bunky Hilstrom with a light comedic touch. The WAC is engaged in a battle of the sexes with the Army's condescending attitude toward female soldiers. The proving ground is competitive field maneuvers with the Army.

Musicals and light-headed charmers were perfect ways to present man-hungry woman folk as worthy of their prey. "What good is a woman without a man?" is a question that defines the lives, fates and reputations of women in two different eras.

In *The Second Greatest Sex* and *Ain't Misbehavin'*, the American West and America in the '50s may be separated by a century, but the power schemes are the same and women illustrate that they always had the power of the vote. For Birdie and Jackie, a snared parson and an old man that gets away are the turnabouts of the mating rituals of the rural and urban ages.

Mamie's next role was in one of Hollywood's first rock 'n' roll movies: *Running Wild*. It tells the story of a carjacking ring and has a soundtrack that includes "Razzle Dazzle" by Bill Halley and the Comets. At first, Mamie was reluctant to do the movie because its black-and-white format was a comedown from her two previous movies, lighthearted musicals made in color.

In retrospect, *Running Wild* is a career highlight, not only because it was at the vanguard of the rock 'n' roll musical craze, but also because it is a spit-and-polish crime drama. Mamie plays Irma Bean, a devil's advocate that looks and acts like a bobbysoxer. Bean is a jitterbugging teen having good times with a member of a carjacking outfit. She is part-blonde airhead scripted by U-I writers, but also foreshadows the bold antagonists that exemplify Mamie Van Doren's best years at MGM with Albert Zugsmith.

Mamie's roles for U-I were mainly light comedic parts. For her type that meant voluptuous and dumb. Irma Bean was a rebel, but she was no quick thinker. Ellen Ballard, her last role for the studio, was a departure from her other parts. It is no surprise because the producer is Albert Zugsmith, the maverick producer who would later showcase Mamie Van Doren in all her glory in a series of sharp satires and lurid melodramas for MGM, Allied Artists and Universal-International during the last year of its merger.

In 1956, Universal-International began to scale down its roster and the hopefuls that never matured

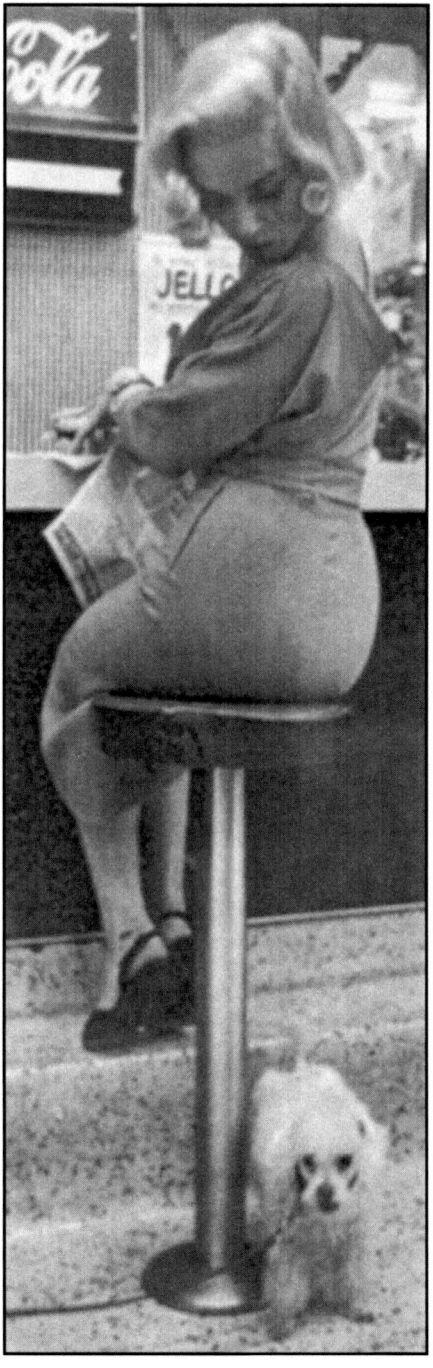

An early publicity shot of Mamie, playing up the Marilyn angle. 1953, Movie Pin-Ups.

A striking shot of Mamie Van Doren reclining. 1955, Universal Pictures Company, Inc.

to stardom were the ones to be let go. Another era was ending for the studio and a change was due with the approaching decade. U-I cancelled its contract with Mamie the same year when she started a family with her husband, Ray Anthony, the trumpet player-bandleader-actor. A studio representative cited motherhood was inconsistent with her screen type. It was an absurd decision considering that her next phase included many roles that were anything but motherly. *Star in the Dust* brought an end to Mamie's apprenticeship in one of the last movie guilds of the old order.

Van Doren moved away from the studio peroxide blonde bombshell after she parted ways with Universal-International. From 1957 to 1959, she created a series of rock 'n' roll bad girls and star-crossed crime molls in pictures by Howard W. Koch, Albert Zugsmith and Edward L. Cahn. A mixture of creative styles and slants on her old image gave Mamie Van Doren a chance to reinvent herself. She lampooned her old style with roles in *The Girl in Black Stockings* ('57), *Teacher's Pet* ('58) and the Italian-made *The Beautiful Legs of Sabrina* ('58).

Van Doren portrayed different types of ingénues in three films directed by Howard W. Koch. She had a supporting part in *The Girl in Black Stockings* and a starring role in the harsh *Untamed Youth*, a cotton plantation rock n' roll drama. The next year she starred in *Born Reckless*.

Although the subject matter and tone of the films couldn't be more disparate, they shared a shadow-laden look because of Koch's dark style. *The Girl in Black Stockings* is a lurid low-key murder mystery set in a Utah vacation resort. *Untamed Youth* is a brutal incarcerated youth film with strange themes and sordid characters. Every so often, the sadism erupts into rock 'n' roll song-and-dance numbers. *Born Reckless* is a rodeo romance with a rockabilly score and sideshow equestrian performances.

Mamie literally polishes off her wide-eyed curvaceous blonde doll in the murder mystery. She creates a bold rock 'n' roll rebel for the plantation movie and plays a singing rodeo performer who ropes the steers in the nightclubs and on the rodeo circuit.

Untamed Youth and *Born Reckless* are musicals, but they are not the cute and fuzzy ones Mamie made at Universal-International. In the Warner Brothers' dramas, marrying a millionaire and teaching the town men folk a lesson in bedside manners did not mean the same thing they did at her old lot. The closest thing she came to grit and filth at U-I was *Running Wild*, the chop-shop movie with the rock 'n' roll soundtrack.

1958 was a year that showed the variety of Mamie Van Doren's movies. Besides starring in *Born Reckless*, she starred in the Italian-made romantic comedy *The Beautiful Legs of Sabrina* and had a part in *Teacher's Pet*, starring Clark Gable and Doris Day. She also headlined a cabaret act in Las Vegas with a style that was showcased on Steve Allen's variety show and appearances on her husband's program, *The Ray Anthony Show*.

In 1959, Mamie signed with Imperial Pictures to do *Guns, Girls and Gangsters* and *Vice Raid*, both sleekly directed by Edward L. Cahn. They are slim and fast crime dramas streamlined and packed with unsavory characters with big ambitions. A tragic body count and scarred survivors are part of Cahn's way of doing things.

Vi Victor and Carol Hudson are blondes whose broadsides are the things that hook shady power mongers. In the world of Victor and Hudson, the gangsters are violent dukes who seek to enlarge their fiefdoms. In both instances, the women are the keys to the schemes that will net ill fortunes.

It was typical of the world her characters lived in during her post-U.I. Years. That was especially true for the Albert Zugsmith years, the antitheses of corporate-sponsored television land.

Few producers mined the exploitation genre better than Albert Zugsmith. His films may appeal to the lowest common denominator of emotions, but they are sharp-witted satires of cherished American values. Zugsmith's productions started with *Captive Women* ('52) and ended with *Sappho, Darling* ('69). They ranged from the lowbrow *Fanny Hill* ('64) and *The Incredible Sex Revolution* ('65) to the brilliant *Touch of Evil* ('57) by Orson Welles and the bizarre *Confessions of an Opium Eater* ('62), starring Vincent Price, which Zugsmith directed.

Lillith is the harem's prize, a Euro-blonde with a subservient charm that brings liberation in revolution. 1954, Universal Pictures Company, Inc.

Danni Crayne (l) and Mamie Van Doren (r) rehearse a musical number from *Ain't Misbehavin'*. 1955, Universal Pictures Company, Inc.

Universal-International signed Zugsmith in 1955 to produce *Female on the Beach*, Joan Crawford's comeback film. It did nothing to jumpstart Crawford's career, but led to a series of pulp thrillers and a couple of classics: *The Tattered Dress* ('57), *Slaughter on Tenth Ave.* ('57), *The Incredible Shrinking Man* ('57), *Touch of Evil* ('58), and *High School Confidential* ('58).

Over the years, Zugsmith worked with directors like Jack Arnold, Charles F. Haas, Hugo Haas, Harry Keller and Orson Welles to turn American icons into gems from hell. Some of the actors who wielded power in these hells were Dan Duryea, Walter Matthau, Mickey Rooney, Mel Welles and Norman "Woo Woo" Grabowski.

Zugsmith's hells were also blessed by the sultry presence of Mamie Van Doren, Janet Leigh, and Hedy Lamarr or a legion of starlets like Irish McCalla, Yvette Mimieux, Gloria Talbott, and Tuesday Weld.

He had the showman's knack of using gimmicks like hiring the siblings of screen legends to appear in his films. Credits included Charles Chaplin, Jr., Harold Lloyd, Jr., and John Drew Barrymore. Legends of the past were also given their due and this included Louis Armstrong, Walther Winchell, Rocky Marciano and Jackie Coogan.

The best of Van Doren's roles are her collaborations with Albert Zugsmith. Mamie signed with Albert Zugsmith and MGM in 1958 for a series of films that would redefine her style. Zugsmith's intense formula was enhanced by Mamie's presence and she was not cheapened by the seediness of his movies; in fact, she illuminated them with her vigor.

Starting with 1958's *High School Confidential* and ending with *College Confidential* in 1960, Mamie Van Doren and Albert Zugsmith explored the dark side of the Fifties and examined the problems to be dealt with in the Sixties. Zugsmith's sleaze quotient and Van Doren's dynamism made these movies unique exploitation treats.

In *High School Confidential*, a potboiler about a high-school drug ring, directed by Jack Arnold, Auntie Gwen takes a bite of the forbidden fruit and winds up with an Adam's apple. Mamie is billed as a guest star and her part is supportive, but memorable. She plays a part that stretches the boundaries of taboo yet gets the rubber stamp of approval by the film's finale.

High School Confidential is Albert Zugsmith's blend of rock 'n' roll and the drug menace. Marijuana is the forbidden weed that has been driving clean-cut kids to the hard stuff. Wise guy juveniles and shady adults are headaches of the straight-arrow upright types menaced by the new youth culture. The innocent victims are the future captains of industry and their house-wives-to-be.

Auntie Gwen Dulaine is a shapely and efficient federal program who exploits societal rot to polish the veneer of public decency. She plays it crooked for entrapment's sake, but winds up joining the triumphant trio at the end of the movie. Along the way, she leads the decency police on, only to flash her badge in their faces and make them apologize for their dirty minds.

Georgia Altera is the checkmate prize for a rapist and a macho cop in *The Beat Generation,* Zugsmith's sordid riff on beatniks, misogyny, and the subterranean world of the nuclear generation. Altera's hell is that

Auntie Gwen doesn't take no for any answer, not even from her nephew (Russ Tamblyn), in *High School Confidential.* 1958, Loew's Inc.

German press book cover for *The Girl In Black Stockings*.
1958, Film Neues Programm.

she is blonde bait for psychos operating on both sides of the law. She thwarts them by remaining resilient in her resistance and succeeds where others have failed in turning the tables on her male predators.

The Beat Generation is about a woman-hating detective's hunt for a rapist and his inability to deal with his wife's entrance into the unholy triangle. Georgia Altera exposes the hypocrisy of sexual identity in '50s America. The cop and the rapist try to define women according to their own perversions. They fail because their prey refuses to become a victim: Georgia Altera is not your stereotypical '50s buxom blonde.

The movie, a morose study of sexual attitudes and societal identities, also includes strained hipster histrionics, bad poetry and songs from hootenannies in Hell, a strangely out-of-place Maxie Rosenbloom as the Wrestling Beatnik and Louis Armstrong and his All-Stars.

In *Girls Town*, Silver Morgan serves a bum rap for a wrongful murder that she had nothing to do with. Valor and principle land her in Girls Town, a Catholic home for wayward girls. She spends her time going up against the system only to embrace it in the end.

Silver Morgan mixes with a Mother Superior, a queen bee who uses judo and the criminal justice system to clear her name and protect her blood. She is clever and it gets her in trouble with her adversaries, but

Mamie Van Doren strikes a lethal pose for *Untamed Youth*.
1957, Warner Bros. Pict. Dist. Corp.

the question of opposites becomes a solution to her problems. Her answered prayer is a reversal of fortune.

Silver Morgan fights to survive in a reformatory run by Catholic nuns who exact repentance from wayward teenagers in *Girls Town*. She fights a battle on two fronts: the disciplinarian nuns and a vigilante goon squad of other girls. Dead man's curves and a chest full of breathe cause more trouble than the delinquent teens. Morgan takes everyone on and wins in the end when she spits in the face of the system that tries to railroad her.

In *The Big Operator*, suburban heaven becomes a torture chamber for an aw-shucks! family of postwar America. Mary Gibson is the All American Girl Next Door who married the Average Guy from down the block. Her world is turned upside down when her husband and son become victims in a brass-knuckled overture of graft, torture and murder.

The Big Operator is a hard-hitting crime drama whose blows are all beneath the belt. From the diminutive crime boss with an iron fist to witness immolation and cement truck internment, the characters, action and settings are grim and gross. They smell illicit, even the suburban leads played by Steve Cochran and Mamie Van Doren.

The Gibsons see what is under the belly of the suburban Nirvana they call home. Mary Gibson is a happy housewife-turned-vicious tigress when her husband is tortured by the crooks who have kidnapped her son for an encore. The jungle is a crime lair where her son is held captive by a goon squad. She is victorious in recovering her son from the crime ring.

College Confidential and *The Private Lives of Adam and Eve* were made for Universal-International in the last years of its merger. In between, they made *Sex Kittens Go to College* for Allied Artists. It was a hybrid film, being part college hijack film and stag movie. Sex and sensuality was the theme of the three movies, part of a trend inspired by the impact of The Kinsey Report.

Sally Blake is one of the confused generation of college students in *College Confidential*, a strange mix of Kinsey and smalltime courtroom justice. She uses a sex survey to hide her after-hour hi-jinks and the lie escalates into a scandal. Beauty and esthetics are put on trial and reputations are made and destroyed.

College Confidential is part beach movie and part smooth attempt to tweak the nose of the morals police. *The New York Times* review on August 20, 1960, calls the film "a piece of movie claptrap…a picture best

Clark Gable and Mamie Van Doren between takes on *Teacher's Pet*.
1957, Perlsea Company and Paramount Pictures Corp.

described as punk." Mamie is described as "that pneumatic drill leftover from *High School Confidential*." It ends by fearing that Zugsmith may launch "a new 'Confidential' vehicle" like "a loud rusty engine."

Instead, he gave them Eve as the mother of all things in *The Private Lives of Adam and Eve* and *Sex Kittens Go to College* showcasing Professor Mathilda West, a genius who modifies behavior and not intellect.

In *Sex Kittens Go to* College, Professor West is a genius whose sexuality is more powerful than her I.Q. It wreaks havoc at Collins College, where she electrifies the faculty and the student body with her mind-bending assets. The degrees of beauty stifle everyone who comes in contact with her. It is her downfall and her descent gives rise to the rebirth of the other women as Prof. West clones with finite dimensions.

The fall of mankind is a burlesque skit where the Devil is an icon who lays it on thick in *The Private Lives of Adam and Eve*. Temptation is the bane of domesticity and the forbidden fruit is a snack on the side. Eve is the mother of guilt and she gets to prove it in a tour-de-force

Vi Victor is reluctantly drawn into an ill-fated armored-car heist in *Guns, Girls and Gangsters*. 1958, United Artists Corp.

Introduction: A Montage of Inamoratas   37

Vi Victor's torrid dance pose is highlighted on the cover of Glance Magazine's issue on sex in America. 1958, Glance Publications.

confessional in the rain where lightning is a shower of gold and Adam's rib becomes a pat on the stomach.

Both characters are two perfect complements of the Blonde Sexpot of Western Civilization. The genius and the visionary can be switched and still have relevance in each other's tale. The professor could be condemned by history for the fall of mankind because of her genius and Eve's unique sexuality could cause a disturbance among campus youth.

Each decade's identity is like a hangover that lasts a couple of years into the next era. Old styles continue until they merge or are eclipsed by the new outlook. It usually occurs as the midpoint approaches. A couple of more years of milking the old looks and attitudes was a safe haven for many of the contract players of the old studio system. For Van Doren and Albert Zugsmith, the last wave included *College Confidential, Sex Kittens Go to College* and *The Private Lives of Adam and Eve.*

Hollywood was undergoing drastic change, along with the rest of America. Styles, attitudes and images lost their luster as the system that nurtured them slowly became obsolete. In 1961, Mamie traveled to Argentina to make *The Blonde from Buenos Aires*, a comedy with Jean-Pierre Aumont.

Steamy shot for a photo layout in The Girl Watcher magazine. 1957, Girlwatcher.

Introduction: A Montage of Inamoratas 39

Mamie Van Doren plays Prof. Vera West, a Renaissance woman, in *Sex Kittens Go To College.* 1960, Allied Artists.

She returned to the United States and was to star in *Kiss Her Goodbye,* about a mentally-challenged nineteen-year-old with the mind of an eight-year-old child. Financing fell through so she kept busy by performing in theater and cabaret. There was also a return to the tube to fill the void.

In *The Candidate* and *3 Nuts in Search of a Bolt*, a swan song and a fan dance become the same thing. They are independent features made at a time when the old studio system was giving up the ghost. MCI had acquired Universal-International and change was rampant at other studios, too.

To old school purists, Van Doren's appearances in *The Candidate* and *3 Nuts in Search of a Bolt* are scandalous descents into hell because of their sordid subject matter. The same mentality that judged her rock 'n' roll melodramas had their final say about her closing credits as the blonde vamp. The irony is that *The Candidate* and *3 Nuts in Search of a Bolt* would have been bold counter-culture classics if they were made in the late '60s or early '70s. To popularize *3 Nuts in Search of a Bolt,* Mamie had a spread in the February issue of *Playboy* magazine.

1964 signaled the closing round for all things Fifties when Beatlemania introduced a new sound and attitude. Carnaby Street was fashionable and the Fifties look was officially a joke. The stars of yesteryear had to figure out a way to deal with the new way of doing things.

When the '60s found its personality, it was vitriolic and nihilistic. It considered itself autonomous and dismissed the past as being plastic and useless. The changing of value systems created a cynical filtration criterion that either accepted or neutralized idols of the Fifties.

Glamour and veneer no longer counted because the truth was deeper than the surface. The Sixties narcissistic superiority complex pronounced the Fifties as being superficial and without redeeming benefits. It is ironic because beatniks and rock 'n' roll were vital to the formation of part of the Sixties counter-culture. After the changes came, those who didn't stay and adapt or accept early retirement resuscitated their careers overseas.

A need to stay relevant was the clarion call and the first step was to sweep clean the Hollywood constellation. It was a time when stars worked in television or migrated overseas. Many of the supporting players and bit part actors and actresses became stars in the new Hollywood.

As their stars shone, the remnants of the Universal-International star system were either working in television, starring in potboilers overseas or had become inactive. If recovery didn't occur by the Seventies, it was parodies on network television or embarrassing roles in lurid independent drive-in movies.

For Mamie, it was another trans-Atlantic trip, this time for a Teutonic Western. *The Sheriff Was a Lady* is a revenge Western, although not along the lines of *A Star in the Dust.* It isn't because Beba Loncar plays the sheriff instead of John Agar or the music is rock 'n' roll instead of

Saxie Symbol plies the lost art of the striptease in *3 Nuts In Search of a Bolt*. 1964, Harlequin Int. Pictures.

acoustic ballads. Both films are strange, only *The Sheriff Was a Lady* is funny and *A Star in the Dust* is grim. In the West German Western, Mamie is a dance hall queen who sings a couple of songs in a saloon and sets up the bad guy for a hard fall.

The Hollywood of her glory years no longer existed and theater is where Mamie kept her chops sharp performing in *Gentleman Prefer Blondes, Silk Stockings, Will Success Spoil Rock Hunter?* and *How to Suc-*

Movie herald for *The Beat Generation*, a deranged crime thriller with the Zugsmith touch. 1959, Loew's Inc.

ceed in Business Without Really Trying. There were also musical revues at Latin Quarter in New York and the Thunderbird Hotel in Las Vegas from 1964 to 1966.

It was a matter of time before the bargain basement producers came calling. Van Doren's roles in Limbo are now cult favorites, but, at the time, they were part of the closing attractions of the shrinking drive-in circuit.

Nurse Nora Hall battles carnivorous plants in *The Navy vs. the Night Monsters.* The movie is based on Murray Leinster's book, *The Earth's End.* The original title was *The Night Crawlers* and it clocked in at eighty minutes. There are no monsters in the first version by director Michael Hoey. The producers added new footage with the Triffid-like monsters to officially make it a monster movie. Mamie makes the grade as a nurse who helps to successfully destroy the Antarctic flesh-eating mobile trees in a climactic battle in the jungle.

Moana is the leader of sea Amazons who worship a rubber pterodactyl in *Voyage to the Planet of Prehistoric Women.* They have mental powers that can melt the landscape. The Amazons-on-the-beach footage

Poster for *Girls Town*, a rock and roll movie set in a Catholic reformatory for girls. 1959, Loew's Inc.

Saxie Symbol is a bitter, disillusioned stripper who uses self-hatred as a weapon of choice in *3 Nuts in Search of a Bolt*. 1964, Harlequin Int. Pictures.

is tacked onto a Russian sci-fi movie, *Storm Planet*. The producer is Roger Corman and Peter Bogdanovich directs and narrates under the name Derek Thomas.

The Las Vegas Hillbillys pairs Mamie Van Doren and Jayne Mansfield as Boots Malone and the larger-than-life Tawny. The former '50s rivals meet without doing any scenes together. It is the magic of editing and equal credits. All for what amounts to a Ferlin Husky country music special with many of the genre's stars performing their hits.

Old feuds and cult status became moot with the shocking and rueful death of Jayne Mansfield shortly after the movie was released. Van Doren's last bond with Mansfield shares a strange connection to the past. Mamie was starring in a version of *Gentlemen Prefer Blondes* at The Wedgeworth Theater in Glen Cove, Long Island. It was one of Marilyn Monroe's most notable roles.

The play was held over because of popular acclaim and this conflicted with its opening in Biloxi. The compromise was hiring Mansfield to play the role until Mamie was finished in Drury Lane. It is ironic that Marilyn Monroe was the last link between Mamie Van Doren and Jayne Mansfield. Their final encounter was at a party where they admitted to each other that the era of the blonde superstar was finished.

Mrs. Hathaway is a case in point in *How to Be Smart,* an obscure low-budget comedy about a juvenile country preacher who goes to Los Angeles to save it from sin. Mamie has three short scenes as a television's sponsor's daughter, a pampered temptress. *How to be Smart* is a revival tent show traveling the dying circuit of rural drive-ins. It was the Sixties, when everything was being turned upside down. Tradition was being trampled and here was a slice of an Americana morality play with Mamie Van Doren as Jezebel. *How to Be Smart* is a movie that would have gotten the stamp of approval from the Legion of Decency.

Introduction: A Montage of Inamoratas 45

Mamie headlines the bill for Monte Prosner's *All New Ziegfeld Follies of 1965*. 1965, Hotel Thunderbird.

In 1967, Mamie opened the New Year with a week on *Hollywood Squares*, a nightly game show hosted by Peter Marshall. Like all shows of its type, *Hollywood Squares* was part shrine to the stars of yesterday's Hollywood. Many of them stopped by to reconnect with a television audience that remembered them from the movies of their youth.

Mamie traveled to Vietnam for the first time to visit the troops and bolster morale. In her autobiography, she recounts the bleak and maddening experiences of visiting the beaten paths of the war zone, places where even the USO shows did not venture.

The Sixties may have had a bitter disposition toward actresses and actors from the Fifties, but the Seventies made up for it by having a split personality. The big screen was contemptuous of most of the players from the Fifties, who worked mostly in obscure independent films or drive-in cheapies. Television, on the other hand, had an almost reverential attitude toward the stars of yesteryear.

Much of '70s television was a glorification of the '50s film industry. Many former screen stars found steady work on television along with directors, writers and producers. A few stars had shows of their own and other '50s icons had a reserved reverent status with nostalgia-based programs like *Fantasy Island* and *The Love Boat*. They also commanded respect on variety and interview shows. Mamie's '70s credits reflect the decade's split personality.

In 1971, she had a supporting part as the svelte Sharon Miller, a frontier beauty, in the execrable Filipino Western *The Arizona Kid*. It starred Chaquito, the famous Filipino comedian, in a revenge tale not unlike *The Sheriff Was a Lady*. If a West German Western seems absurd, try to imagine a Filipino Western comedy-revenge tale. The premise is ludicrous and the result is incongruous. It comprises an odd bookend for *Star in the Dust* and *The Sheriff Was a Lady*.

It still remains a mystery how Van Doren could not find work in Hollywood like her Fifties contemporaries. Most of her cohorts may have been working in low-budget quickies, but at least they had marquee value for the second-string exploitation producers. Seeing as how Mamie was always ahead of the curve, it could be that she already had her quickie phase in the Sixties.

After Van Doren's return to the silver screen in *The Arizona Kid*, it was live burlesque revivals like *In One Bed and Out the Other*, *Scandalous Follies*, *Two and Two Make Sex* and *Makin' Whoopee* with Imogene Coca.

Introduction: A Montage of Inamoratas 47

Back cover for Mamie's 70's disco album. 70's, Churchill Records, Ltd.

She served as the mystery guest on *The New What's My Line?* to publicize *Scandalous Follies* at The Wedgeworth Theater.

Mamie may not have been starring on the silver screen, but she still had a place in the hearts of her fans. It is to her credit that she did not rely on her reputation to keep her going. Dinner theater had become popular during that time because it was a place where many older fans could see their big screen idols in person. Then, there was always Las Vegas, if you had what it takes—and Mamie definitely had what it takes to click with the high rollers.

Mamie appeared with Sammy Davis, Jr. at the Las Vegas' Sands Hotel in 1973 for a two-week engagement. It was live entertainment until two years later when she had a part in Moonstone Production's *That Girl from Boston*, an unreleased film by Matt Cimber, who was once married to Jayne Mansfield. The movie also featured Alexandra Hay, as the title character, and George "Buck" Flowers as Thirsty.

A new musical style called disco challenged the popularity of rock 'n' roll in the mid-Seventies. It was all about doing the Hustle and partying to dawn. In 1977, Mamie recorded a disco album, "As in Mamie Van Doren…"

The aftermath of '70s glorification was obsolescence, as the '80s declared all that passed before it non-existent. Instead of being militant, like its narcissistic forebears in the '60s, the '80s tribe practiced greed in business attire. In the '80s, even many of the stars of the '70s were considered has-beens so it should be no surprise that very few people recognized the stars that came before them. That is why it is astounding that Mamie Van Doren defied the odds by having a career resurgence in the '80s.

In 1984, Los Angeles' Nuart Theatre scheduled a revival of her films, hosted by Albert Zugsmith, Aubrey Schenk and Howard W. Koch. It was a popular smash that received media attention and a segment on *Entertainment Tonight*. *Playboy* courted Mamie for another pictorial and she agreed to do it, only to change her mind about having the pictures published for the public.

To capitalize on her return to the spotlight, Rhino Records included some of her songs on a compilation CD called "Va Va Voom! Screen Sirens Sing!," which also included songs by Sophia Loren and Jayne Mansfield. Mamie resumed her recording career with a 12" dance single, "Queen of Pleasure" and "Young Dudes." Its success was followed by "State of Turmoil" and a performance backed by a rock band at the Palomino in North Hollywood. She also served as the Queen of the 1986 Gay Parade.

Mamie hosted a series of juvenile delinquent videos and appeared as herself in documentaries about rock 'n' roll movies or blonde myth studies. Her '80s highlight was her role as Debbie Stockwell, an oversexed college nurse, in the 1986 coming-of-age comedy *Free Ride*. The movie was one of the many kids vs. adult comedies that comprised one of Hollywood's most successful franchises: the teen angst comedy. Mamie

Virginia Mayo, Kathryn Grayson, Maxine Andrews and Mamie Van Doren belt out a classic song for an 80's nostalgia show highlighting the stars of Hollywood's Golden Age. 1980's, ABC Television.

playing a stock role in an adolescent comedy for the '80s generation is what makes the movie special. She also sings "Young Dudes" on the film's soundtrack.

    Her next role was a small part as the alluring madam of an Atlantic City whorehouse in a HBO cable movie called *The Glory Years,* made in 1987. The same year, Mamie wrote *Playing the Field,* her fourth autobiography and it received the tabloid media treatment. Typical of the publicity was *The Star's* headlines: "Once Johnny Carson told her, 'I've had a vasectomy,'" "How Steve McQueen took LSD to make sex better," and "Why she wouldn't say 'yes' to Warren Beatty."

    To help promote the book, Mamie appeared on the *Oprah Winfrey Show* as part of a symposium on white blondes. Other guests included Monique Van Vooren, Barbara Eden and Teri Copley. The hostess did nothing to hide her contempt and sarcasm in general, but lost her composure when she asked Mamie Van Doren about some of the men she knew.

Her candid answer included a couple of stinging comments about two prominent personalities, one of whom was a personal friend of Oprah's. The audience wasn't exactly pleased with Mamie's frankness, starting with her humorous anecdote about a night as Rock Hudson's beard before it turned into a bush over a cup of coffee and spilled beads. It ended with a less than flattering anecdote about Burt Reynolds. Van Doren nonchalantly shrugged off the audience's displeasure by saying, "You can't please everybody."

In 1994, Mamie Van Doren received a star on Hollywood Boulevard and appeared as herself on *Rhyme and Punishment,* the Christmas show of television's *L.A. Law.* Her screenplay, *A Sex Kitten in Vietnam,* was completed in 1996 and entails her tours of Vietnam from 1968-1972.

She launched her celebrated website on Labor Day, 1998. Cyberspace has enabled her to have another resurgence as it tracks the life of the modern Mamie Van Doren. It is part diary, political blog, celebrity profile, portrait gallery and autobiographical trip down memory lane. She has gained a new legion of fans through the website and maintains a personality that is contemporary, not nostalgic.

There were still movie cameos, such as Rita, the owner of a topless bar in *The Vegas Connection,* a made-for-TV movie starring Robert Carradine as Matt Chance, private eye. An outrageous R-rated cameo in *Slackers* (2002), a teen comedy for a new generation, is how she entered the 21st century.

Versatility is the key to Mamie Van Doren's longevity. It is the reason why she survived the Platinum Era and the chrysalis of the Sixties to become a goddess matron to a new generation of man-eaters and empire builders via cyberspace and a glorifying website.

Jet Pilot

Jet Pilot: (1949[released 1957]-RKO-112 min.)
Colonel Shannon: John Wayne. *Anna:* Janet Leigh. *Major General Black:* J.C. Flippen. *Major Rexford:* Paul Fix. *George Rivers:* Richard Rober. *Colonel Sokolov:* Roland Winters. *Colonel Matoff:* Hans Conried. *Uncredited:* Joan Olander (Mamie Van Doren). *Director:* Josef von Sternberg. *Screenplay and Producer:* Jules Furthman. *Cinematography:* Philip G. Cochran, Winton C. Hoch. *Editors:* Michael R. McAdam and Harry Marker. *Music:* Bronislau Kaper.

Cold War politics was a reality of the post-WW II world. The USA and the USSR emerged from the war as enemies in a continental struggle that included war and propaganda. In 1949, *Jet Pilot* was made in the spirit lampooning the confrontation with an East-meets-West love affair. Colonel Shannon (John Wayne) is an Air Force officer who is assigned to escort Anna (Janet Leigh), a Soviet pilot who has defected. She has flown her plane from Siberia and lands at an Alaskan outpost. He falls in love with her, unaware that she is scheming to lure him back to the USSR.

Jet Pilot is proof that your head is in the clouds if you are in love. It is also a truism that opposites attract and there is nothing unusual about that. It is the extent of the opposition and its root cause that makes the contrariety unique, especially if the principals are a Yankee and a Commie in the immediate postwar era.

The comedy's strong point is the contrast between the ideological differences of Capitalism and Communism. Anna is confused yet in-

Poster for Howard Hughes' *Jet Pilot*, released eight years after it was made in 1949. 1957, RKO Pictures, Inc.

trigued by American slang and customs. She is also bemused by a standard of living without rationing. At first, hot and cold running water, private living quarters and fun in the open outdoors reinforces her prejudices about the West as being a decadent civilization. Eventually, the freedom-seeking side of her soul converts her to the American way of life.

Jet Pilot was released eight years after it was made because Howard Hughes, the producer, had to wade through over two thousand hours of footage that needed to be whittled down to a reasonable viewing time.

The Duke (John Wayne) adapts to Cold War politics the old-fashioned way with a hard-line Communist jet pilot played by Janet Leigh. 1957, RKO Pictures, Inc.

The best visuals in the movie are the breathtaking and stunning aerial shots of the bombers during maneuvers. Chuck Yeager performed many of John Wayne's aeronautics and they appear to be animated because they seem so unreal.

John Wayne is the Duke, WWII American icon reinvented for the Cold War. The Duke gets to show his sensitive side in this movie, falling in love with the Russian spy and risking serious disciplinary action and the ruination of his Air Force career.

Janet Leigh was RKO's screen ingénue before she would later gain cult status because of her roles in *Touch of Evil* ('58) and *Psycho* ('60). In *Jet Pilot*, she displays a rare blend of silk and steel in her character. During the Fifties, the few movies that had strong and independent women in key roles were mainly cheap science-fiction films or movies about Communism

Jay C. Flippen and Paul Fix had yet to reach their decrepit and grizzled stage. They still had strength and authority in their roles as a Major General and a Major. Roland Winters and Hans Conried have small parts as Russian officers relishing the thought of breaking Colonel Shannon. Winters winds up in the uranium mines and Conried is his pompous replacement. Joan Olander plays an Air Force cadet who looks up and points at Wayne's plane flying by. *Jet Pilot* was not released until 1957, the height of the anti-domestic Communist crackdown.

Two Tickets To Broadway

Two Tickets To Broadway: (1951 - RKO - 106 min.-C) *Dan Carter:* Tony Martin. *Nancy Peterson:* Janet Leigh. *Hannah Holbrook:* Gloria DeHaven. *Lew Conway:* Eddie Bracken. *Joyce Campbell:* Ann Miller. *Director:* James V. Kern. *Screenplay:* Sammy Cahn (story) and Hal Kanter. *Cinematography:* Edward Conjager, Harry J. Wild. *Editor:* Harry Marker. *Music:* Walter Scharf.

This saccharine and pep-filled movie has an infectious optimism that mixes goodhearted small-town naiveté and eastside streetwise savvy. There is no shortage of snappy songs and the choreographer is a past-his-prime Busby Berkeley.

The plot is the old tried-and-true musical romance about the small-town girl who gets a jubilant send-off to the city to seek fame and fortune on Broadway. She hooks up with like-minded kooky partners on a bus to the Big Town. A silk-throated Romeo and a scheming buffoon are their dubious aids on the road to success.

It could only happen in a movie about the Great White Way with sincere leads, fancy showgirls and a wily second banana. The only thing is that they don't wind up on Broadway; they find success on Bob Crosby's television show.

Nancy Peterson (Janet Leigh) is the Broadway hopeful from Pelican Falls. A zis-boom-bah!-sendoff energizes the bus trip to New York City. She meets three cynical showbiz vets (Ann Miller, Gloria DeHaven and Barbara Lawrence) on the ride and they form a bond with a steel reserve. For the women, destiny is Dan Carter (Tony Martin), a opera-voiced crooner, and Lew Conway (Eddie Bracken), his shifty agent. The agent's

56   The Films of Mamie Van Doren

hustle turns the ruse into a show that, in spite of itself, winds up a hit on Bob Crosby's program.

Janet Leigh and Tony Martin sing and dance like college sweethearts. Martin has an outstanding voice. Leigh is perfect as the simple

Poster for *Two Tickets to Broadway*, an upbeat musical comedy. 1951, RKO Pictures, Inc.

Tony Martin serenades Janet Leigh in her hostelry while a gaggle of starlets (including Joi Lansing [third from the left]) become mesmerized. 1951, RKO Pictures, Inc.

but beautiful small-town girl. She has the fresh face of country time and the healthy lungs and lithe legs of a big city singer and dancer.

They are aided by plenty of songs and musical numbers. Jule Styne and Leo Robin wrote seven of the songs. "Pelican Falls" is the marching band tribute that sounds like "Reveille" and sends the aspiring actress off to New York. "Baby, You'll Never Be Sorry" is a comical number between Gloria DeHaven and Eddie Bracken. "The Worry Bird" is an excellent romp with Miller, DeHaven and Lawrence in Central Park. For Martin and Leigh, "The Closer You Are" is about love in the rain.

Martin and Leigh perform one classic song from the movie, "Manhattan," by Rodgers and Hart. The choreography is likeable and corny but thoroughly lame by Busby Berkeley's old standards. It is still effective, as the leads work well together and there is a bevy of beauties to fill in for the uninspired moves.

Joi Lansing, Kathleen Case and Joan Shawlee are among the beautiful chorines at the all-girls hostelry. The best thing about the number is how it switches from the rooming house for actresses to Central Park, where Martin and Leigh put a head on the song. Joan Olander appears as a bobbysoxer in Bob Crosby's studio during a rehearsal break. Another future star who appears in the scene is Mara Corday.

Smith and Dale, the famed vaudeville comedy team, have supporting roles as the owners of The Palace Deli, the place where everybody meets. The parts were originally intended for Laurel and Hardy but Stan Laurel became ill. The comic masters were scrapped from the project and replaced by the original Sunshine Boys.

Footlight Varieties

Footlight Varieties: (1951-RKO-60 min.)
Stars: Leon Errol, The Sportsmen, Liberace, Jerry Murad's Harmonicats, Frankie Carle Orchestra, Red Buttons, Inesita, Buster West, Mellissa Mason, Jack Paar and Joan Olander (Mamie Van Doren). *Directors:* D.W. Griffith, Benjamin Stoloff and Hal Yates. *Writers:* Felix Adler, D.W. Griffith and Hal Yates. *Producer:* George Bilson. *Cinematography:* J. Roy Hunt and Frank Redmond. *Editors:* Edward W. Williams and Jay Whittredge.

Footlight Varieties has a curio value because of its antique vaudeville format. It is a one-hour showcase of stars, emerging stars, has-beens and never-was'. It is a Saturday matinee squeezed into one movie. There are comedy sketches, musical numbers and novelty bits guided by three directors: D.W. Griffith, Benjamin Stoloff and Hal Yates.

The movie is the third in a line of all-star musical revues for RKO, an attempt by the studio to duplicate the popularity of the form during the wartime era. *Variety Time* ('48) and *Make Mine Laughs* ('49) were filled with stock footage, unlike *Footlight Varieties*, which had new acts, if not fresh material.

D.W. Griffith is the *auteur* of *Confidence*. A far cry from his revolutionary silent movies like *Intolerance* and *The Birth of a Nation,* this short brings his long career to a close. Benjamin Stoloff helms the variety show with Liberace, Red Buttons, The Frankie Carle Orchestra and Jerry Murad and the Harmonicats. Exotic dancing heats up the screen with Inesita, the gypsy dancer.

60   The Films of Mamie Van Doren

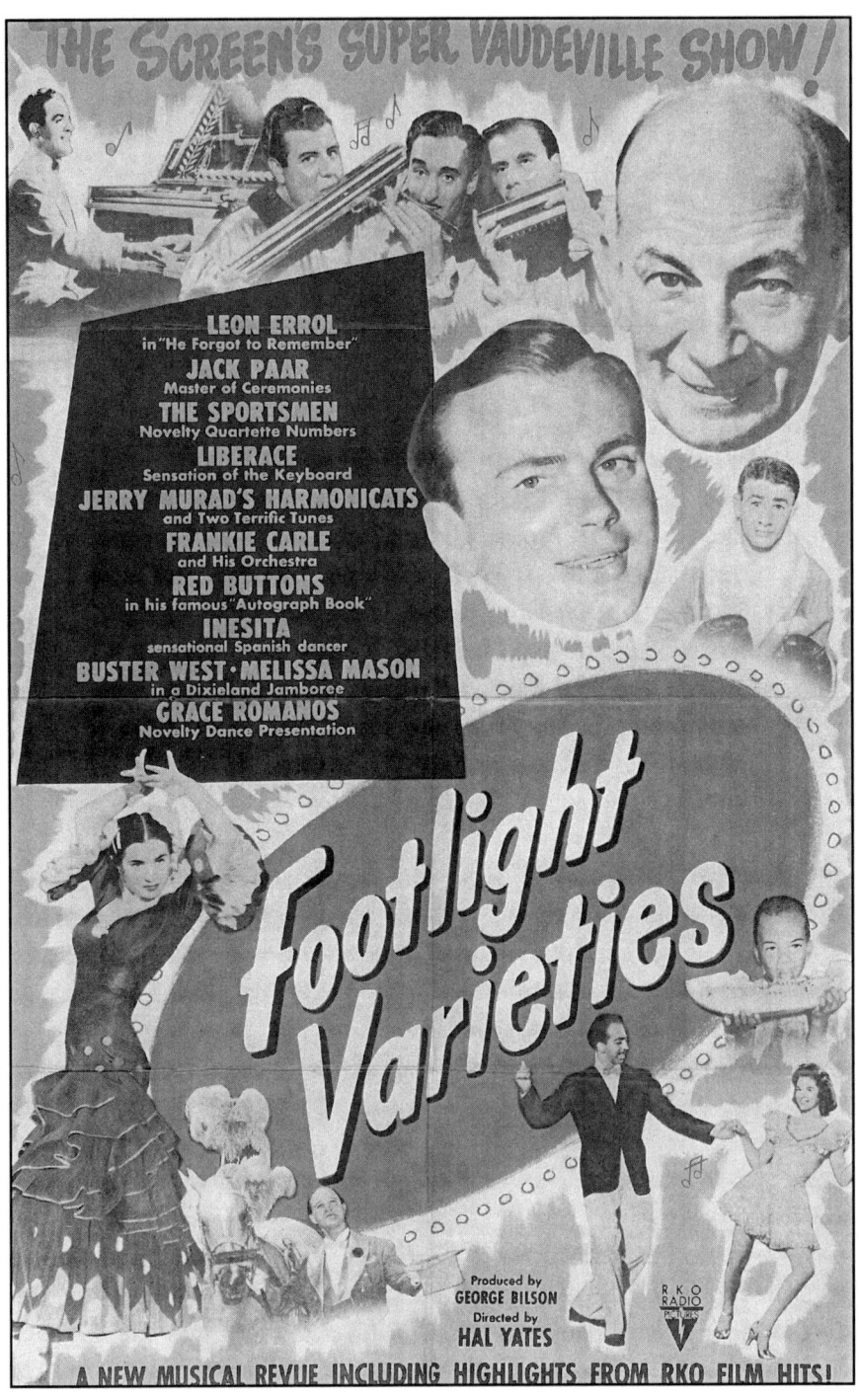

Poster for *Footlight Varieties*. 1951, RKO Pictures, Inc.

Inescita gyrates for the audience. 1951, RKO Pictures, Inc.

The Sportsmen have their moment in the spotlight before being claimed by obscurity. 1951, RKO Pictures, Inc.

The slapstick comedy is provided by Leon Errol in *He Forgot to Remember*, a two-reel comedy. Errol was a knockabout rubber-legged comedian who was famous for his circular drunken duck walk. The comedy is directed by Hal Yates and also stars Dorothy Granger, who played Errol's wife in a series of two-reel comedies in the late '40s.

One of Richard Fleisher's *Flicker Flashbacks*, *Radio City Revels of 1937* bits and *Carle Comes Calling*, a short musical, round out the bill. Jack Paar is the recalcitrant emcee who concludes the movie by necking with Joan Olander in front of a movie screen.

His Kind of Woman

His Kind of Woman: (1951-RKO-120 min.)
Dan Milner: Robert Mitchum. *Lenore Brent/Liz Brady:* Jane Russell. *Nick Ferraro:* Raymond Burr. *Mark Cardigan:* Vincent Price. *Bill Lusk:* Tim Holt. *Thompson:* Charles McGraw. *Helen Cardigan:* Marjorie Reynolds. *Lodge Guest at Bar:* Joan Olander. *Director:* John Farrow and Richard Fleischer (uncredited). *Writers:* Frank Fenton and Jack Leonard. *Executive Producer:* Howard Hughes. *Producer:* Robert Sparks. *Cinematography:* Harry J. Wild. *Editors:* Frederic Knudtson and Eda Warren. *Music Director:* C. Bakaleinikoff. *Songs:* "*You Know*" by Leigh Harline and "*Five Little Miles from San Berdoo*" by Sam Coslow.

His Kind of Woman is a crime drama whose chief interest is the main cast: Robert Mitchum, Jane Russell, Raymond Burr and Vincent Price. Charles McGraw, Jim Backus, Tim Holt, Phillip Van Zandt and Anthony Caruso are the familiar faces that back them up in supporting parts.

Nick Ferraro (Raymond Burr) is a mobster who has been deported to Italy from the United States and bristles over the loss of his two-million-dollar-a-year crime empire. He plans to regain it by trading places with Dan Milner (Robert Mitchum), a lone wolf who won't be missed by anyone once he is gone. The trade will be made through

Jane Russell sings one of two songs in *His Kind of Woman*.
1951, RKO Pictures, Inc.

plastic surgery with the mobster replacing the mark who will be disposed of in international waters. It appears to be a foolproof plan except that Milner is no dope and upsets the scheme with a pigheaded resistance that results in a comedy of errors.

The movie's tone changes too much to make it a successful crime *noir*. The gangland elements are true to the B-movie crime format. The sequence at the Mexican lodge is listless except for a few interesting oddball characters. The climax has mixed results because comedic elements collide with a genuine free-for-all that results in the shooting death of Ferraro by Milner. This proves problematic because the star's glory is stolen by a ham actor who is there for comic relief.

Robert Mitchum plays the atypical crime-drama bad-luck loner. The only thing missing from his wardrobe is a dark cloud over his head. Milner is a dogged man whose string of bad luck is imposed on him by Ferraro through his stateside subordinates. The lone wolf becomes a clay pigeon through a series of mishaps.

Raymond Burr had an established reputation as a big-screen villain before he became Perry Mason, television's most celebrated criminal law-

Robert Mitchum and Jane Russell burn up each other as a reluctant couple drawn into a criminal conspiracy. 1951, RKO Pictures, Inc.

yer. Cold-eyed sadism was his forte and his imposing bulk drove home the point, much to the dismay of his unfortunate victims.

Jane Russell plays Lenore Brent, a bored society doll who hides a secret: she is really Liz Brady, a singer who is trying to make it as a gold digger. She has her sights on an actor at the Mexican lodge where most of the drama takes place. Russell sings two songs, "Five Little Miles from San Berdoo" and "You'll Know." Her charms are enough to rile the local males and she is dangerous to deal with. She has the power to upset the balance of the scales, such as when she sees Ferraro's henchmen kidnap Milner before she enlists the aid of the ham actor, Mark Cardigan (Vincent Price.)

Cardigan is the movie's hero, a blasé actor who turns courageous captain in an assault on Ferraro's ship to rescue Milner. Price hams it up as the screen actor who gallantly leads an attack that ends with Ferraro's death. His performance may be the highlight of the movie, but it upsets the tone and ruins the crime-drama element

Joan Olander has small part as a lodge guest who attends a screening of actor Mark Cardigan's latest movie.

Forbidden

Forbidden: (1953-Universal-International-85 min.) *Eddie Darrow:* Tony Curtis. *Christine Lawrence:* Joanne Dru. *Justin Keet:* Lyle Bettger. *Cliff Chalmer:* Marvin Miller. *Allen Chung:* Victor Sen Yung. *Sam:* Peter Mamakos. *Barney Pendleton:* Alan Dexter. *Mai Tai Sing:* Mai Tai Sing (Soo Lee). *Director:* Randolph Mate. *Screenplay:* Gil Doud. *Story:* William Sackheim. *Producer:* Ted Richmond. *Cinematography:* William H. Daniels. *Editor:* Edward Curtis. *Music:* Frank Skinner. "*You Belong To Me*" by Pee Wee King, Chilton Price and Redd Stewart.

Eddie Darrow (Tony Curtis) is hired by a big city hood named Barney Pendleton (Alan Dexter) to retrieve his girlfriend, Christine Lawrence (Joanne Dru). He makes it seem like love, but it is really her incriminating knowledge of his illicit business affairs. The gangster's errant moll is also Darrow's ex-lover. He tracks her to Macao, where an exotic twist of fate changes things for everyone involved.

Complications arise when Darrow saves the life of Justin Keet (Lyle Bettger), the new mob boss in his old flame's life. Darrow deters an assassination attempt outside of The Lisbon Club, which the gangster owns. Keet shows his gratitude to Darrow with praise, amenities and a job patrolling the floor of his club.

The generosity is caution on Keet's behalf, a way to keep an eye on the new stranger who shares a past with his girlfriend. Polite tension dominates the triangle as intrigue and double dealings involve them in a drama that ends with a new identity for everybody.

68   The Films of Mamie Van Doren

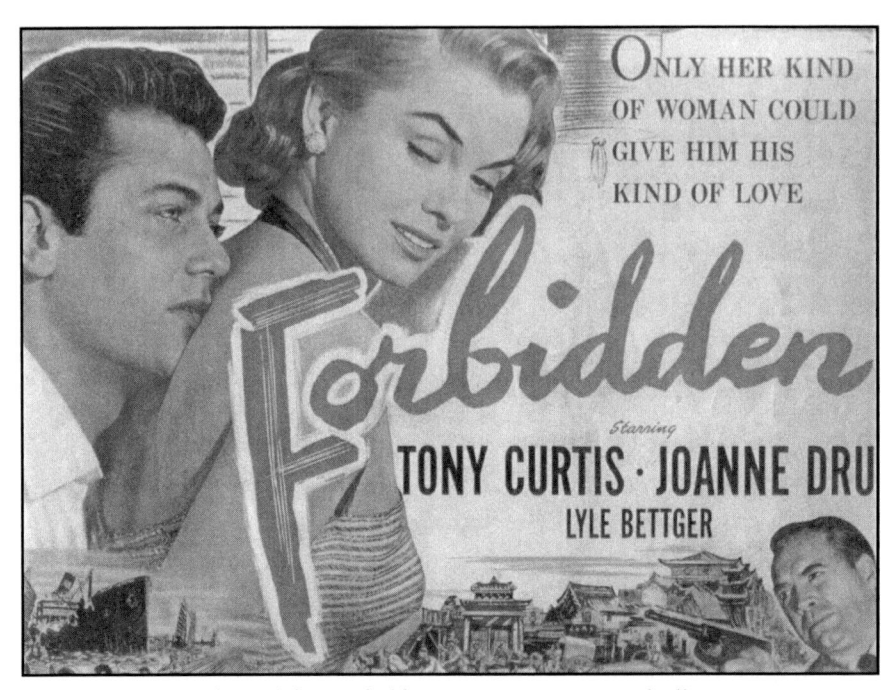

Title card for *Forbidden,* an exotic romantic thriller.
1953, Universal Pictures Company, Inc.

Christine Lawrence (Joanne Dru) and Eddie Darrow (Tony Curtis) are former lovers whose paths mysteriously cross in Asia. Victor Sen-Yung (r) is Eddie's music guru.   1953, Universal Pictures Company, Inc.

Forbidden is an overwrought drama of love, betrayal and a past that becomes the future. Overkill by *leitmotif* does not help, but an explosive ending does. Some of the staples that make the movie work are the love triangle, exotic locale, philosophical piano player and the gambling casino run by a shady expatriate.

A script full of cliché-ridden speeches becomes unbearable at times because of the actors' inability to make the clichés believable. Tony Curtis is a charmer, but his promises of love are crowded out by the *leitmotif*, which is the chorus of the song, "You Belong to Me." The point of Eddie and Christine being the true match has already been established, but the chorus is constantly played, wrapped in a weepy violin. The music reminds the viewer that they are meant for each other. It happens throughout the movie.

Mamie Van Doren made her Universal-International debut singing *You Belong to Me*. 1953, Universal Pictures Company, Inc.

Joanne Dru is strange in a tormented sort of way. Is it her discovery by Darrow or her life as the woman of a Macao crime boss? It does not take her long to fall for Darrow and betray Keet after an impromptu wedding to spite her ex-lover.

Lyle Bettger must be related to the Cheshire Cat because of his keyboard smile. It is disturbing and he displays it often. It is cat and mouse between him and Curtis, all while balancing his rivalries with local foes.

Victor Sen Yung plays Allan Chung, a Yale graduate who plays the piano and waxes philosophical in the Lisbon Club. He is Darrow's conscience and aids him in his final plan. The philosopher plays his music and educates Darrow in the art of rational thinking.

Marvin Miller plays Cliff Chalmer, the shadow who sports a phony city accent and meets a demise engineered by his own stupidity. Peter Mamakos is good as Sam, a bodyguard whose last hit is an exploding ship at sea. Mai Tai Sing is a sexy cigarette girl.

Mamie makes her U-I debut as a sultry chanteuse singing "You Belong to Me" in a nightclub scene where the three principals sit at the same table for the first time. The lyrics and the awkward stares establish a basis for the *leitmotif*.

The All American

The All American: (1953-Universal-International-83 min.) *Nick Benelli*: Tony Curtis. *Sharon Wallace*: Lori Nelson. *Susie Ward*: Mamie Van Doren. *Howard Carter*: Richard Long. *Zip Parker*: Stuart Whitman. *Whizzer*: Jimmy Hunt. *Stan Pomeroy*: Frank Gifford. *Director*: Jesse Hibbs. *Producer*: Screenplay: D.D. Beauchamp. *Story*: Leonard Freeman. *Cinematography*: Maury Gertsman. *Editor*: Edward Curtiss.

The All American is a story where college football is the setting for big stakes glory or ignominious ostracism. Nick Benelli (Tony Curtis) is a troubled All American trying to make a new start as an architecture student at Sheridan University after he leaves his legend and football glory at his alma mater over a betrayal of trust.

At Sheridan, he comes up against school tradition, stuffy professors and elite peer pressure. The battle of wits between Benelli and Howard Carter (Richard Long) is a class reunion where the immigrant son mixes it up with Ivy League green. Benelli challenges the WASP social order as bluebloods suffer punches in the noses and false testimony damages reputations.

The Big Game is always the focal point of movies about collegiate frat boys. Benelli's refusal to play on the team is cited as reverse snobbery; it is not until his secret is revealed to Sarah Wallace (Lori Nelson), a wholesome girl-next-door type of yore, that things begin to change.

The class rivalry extends to the off-limits bar, where the tug of war between tradition and winning at all costs is refereed by Susie Ward (Mamie Van Doren), a single-minded waitress intent on marrying one

Nick Benelli (Tony Curtis) tweaks the beaks of the blue bloods by bringing Susie Ward (Mamie Van Doren), a cocktail waitress, to the faculty party. 1953, Universal Pictures Company, Inc.

of the rich football players from the college. She corrupts the errant college students that wander into the forbidden watering hole. The All American uses her to embarrass the swells at a swanky dinner party, but is expelled from the college after a fight with her in the seedy bar.

The bad feelings threaten the big game and it is not until Susie Ward clarifies her testimony that the All American is exonerated, reinstated to the college and makes the winning play after he suits up at the last moment. Her belated clarification makes her a heroine at the club where she was formerly spurned. The football stars carry her out of the room on their shoulders.

Tony Curtis plays the All American convincingly. His street attitude clashes with the snobbish airs of the big money heirs. He also has the strength to deal with the hostility of the football team of his new school. They are not aware of the reason for his abstinence from the game. His refusal to join the team is mistaken for snobbery and they make him pay for his star status.

Lori Nelson is the perky neighbor who knows Benelli's secret: his parents were killed in a highway crash on the way to see him at the Big

The college teams mocks Benelli (Tony Curtis) because of his refusal to play on the team. They think that it's reverse snobbery. 1953, Universal Pictures Company, Inc.

The haunted All American (Tony Curtis) falls in love with Sharon Wallace (Lori Nelson), the wholesome small town girl. 1953, Universal Pictures Company, Inc.

Tony Curis, Lori Nelson, Mamie Van Doren and Richard Long pose for a cast portrait. 1953, Universal Pictures Company, Inc.

Game at his alma-mater. It is her openhearted kindness that guides him back onto the field. Nelson plays her part well and has the perk and spunk of a small-town do-gooder. She even gets Benelli to trade in his pompadour for an Ivy League college cut.

Richard Long plays Howard Carter, Benelli's chief rival. He is the son of a distinguished alumni and falls out of favor with his former comrades because of his scrapes with Benelli. He is actually disgraced because of a Benelli frame and his bitter attitude is blamed on jealousy at being bested by the football legend.

Barney Phillips is Clipper Colton, a win-at-all costs coach whose selfishness embitters Curtis. He uses Benelli to win the big game that causes the football great to drop out and start anew at another university. It has to do with familial obligation, something that was transgressed by Clipper. He withheld the news of his parents' death so Benelli could make the big play to win the game.

Jimmy Hunt, the child actor, plays Whizzer, the quarterback of a team of kids who plays at the park. The boys playing football draw

Benelli out of his self-imposed ban and he joins the fun by showing them pointers about passing and running. The secretary watches this from the park bench where she is eating her lunch, unbeknownst to Benelli.

Mamie plays Susie Ward, the first role to place her in the blonde gold digger category. She is part airhead blonde of the time, but also possesses a dark street sense worthy of a crime-drama paramour. A woman from the other side of the tracks, she shows the frat boys the meaning of love, but would never be brought home to meet the family. Her earthiness is a threat to the sexuality of blue-blood women, although their upper-crust husbands wish that their spouses could rock 'n' roll like her.

This ambiguity is evident at a posh college party that she attends with Nick Benelli. Susie's presence at the party makes the students uncomfortable because she is supposed to be a shadow relegated to the off-limits bar. They ignore her but the same cannot be said of the Dean of Students. He tells her that he has heard about her legend and the boys consider her second only to their love of football.

"Why second place?" she innocently asks. The dean agrees and becomes a target for Susie's amorous advances. The waitress is on a quest to snag a well-heeled husband. Money is what she is after and makes no bones about it. She has no problem snagging candidates because she is the rich boys' introduction to passion, something like the first kiss or the first prom. That is why she asks the dean, "Why second place?"

It is an understandable attitude for a working-class woman to have. She has a chip on her shoulder because of her dubious social role. That is why she searches for the gold; it is her only way of escaping a humdrum life of waiting on tables. The blue-collar life bores her and she longs to trade it in for a life with the bluebloods.

Hawaiian Nights

Hawaiian Nights: (1953-Universal-International-20m) *Stars:* Pinky Lee, Mamie Van Doren, Lisa Gaye, 1953 Miss Universe Contestants, Danny Stewert Orchestra and the Toni Marsh Dancers.

Pinky Lee was a vaudeville baggy pants comic who later became a huge success on 50's kiddie television. 1954, Universal Pictures Company, Inc.

Vaudeville was dead and burlesque was gasping for air. It lingered on in two-reelers, a division of short subject films that would not survive the decade because of television. Ironically, television later sustained the careers of many knockabout clowns; before that happened, many gave it their best for the twilight phase of the fading shorts.

Mamie Van Doren's nod to her showgirl experience was as an extra in *Hawaiian Nights,* a musical two reeler with a South Seas tropical motif. It is a burlesque comedy mixed with hula dance numbers suited to the knockabout technique of Pinky Lee, who would become one of the clowns whose career was sustained by television.

Mamie's island spice is augmented by Lisa Gaye and the Miss Universe contestants of 1953. The tribal chief is played by Ben Chapman, one of the actors who would play the Gill Man in *The Creature from the Black Lagoon.*

The Danny Stewert Orchestra and the Toni Marsh Dancers perform "Minoi Minoi Ay," "Lovely Hula Girl," "Hawaiian Spear Chant," "Kumu in the Muumuu," "Ama Ama," "Nohea" and "Hoku Okalania."

Yankee Pasha

Yankee Pasha: (1954-Universal-International-83 min.-C) *Jason Starbuck:* Jeff Chandler. *Roxana Reil:* Rhonda Fleming. *Lilith:* Mamie Van Doren. *Sultan:* Lee J. Cobb. *Hassan Sendar:* Hal March. *Omar Id-Din:* Bart Roberts (Rex Reason). *Bassan Said:* Philip Van Zandt. *Zamil:* Benny Rubin. *Elias Darby:* Tudor Owen. *Dick Bailey:* Harry Lauter. *Reil:* Forbes Murray. *Richard O'Brien:* Arthur Space. *First Mate Miller:* John Daheim. *Harem Girls:* Christine Martel, Myrna Hansen, Kinuko Ito, Emita Arosemena, Synove Gulbrandson, Alicia Ibanez, Ingrid Mills and Maxine Morgan. *Director:* Joseph Pevney. *Writers:* Joseph Hoffman; Edison Marshall (novel). *Producer:* Howard Christie. *Composers:* Henry Mancini and Henry Lava. *Cinematography:* Carl E. Guthrie. *Editing:* Virgil W. Vogel.

Yankee Pasha is Universal-International's first CinemaScope picture and has the characteristics of the studio's colorful and entertaining costume dramas. It is a sanitized version of white slavery, a grandiose affair played out against the rustic outdoors life of 1800s Salem, Mass., and the sumptuous world of Islamic Morocco.

The plot is a variation on the swashbuckling theme where heroes wooed, charmed and rescued damsels in distress and the sidekicks, villains and henchmen were portrayed by popular character actors of the era.

Rhonda Fleming is a kidnapped prize from New England and Jeff Chandler plays the square-jawed, broad-shouldered Yankee who heads to

Morocco to rescue her. As a player in a high-stakes game of winner take all, the hero fights and defeats a warlord and outwits the sultan in the name of love.

Jason Starbuck (Jeff Chandler) is a westerner who is tiring of the lonely life of trapping in the Adirondacks. His trip to Salem, Mass., is his last sale and he plans to take an ocean voyage to see the world. Unlike most trappers, Starbuck is well-read and the world of words fills in the lonely gaps of outdoors life. Now, he intends to go beyond the words.

In town, Elias Darby (Tudor Owen), a merchant, admires Starbuck's horse and challenges him to race his prize horse for passage to China on one of his merchant ships. The equestrian contest will have far-reaching influence and no one will be the same once it ends in Starbuck's favor.

Before the race, Starbuck is secretly coached in negotiating the course by Roxana (Rhonda Fleming), fiancé of his opponent. Roxana's infidelity leads to public embarrassment, ruined marriage plans, her father's dismissal from her erstwhile husband's firm and relocation in Europe.

Lilith (Mamie Van Doren) exerts her charm and influence on a reluctant Starbuck (Jeff Chandler). 1954, Universal Pictures Company, Inc.

Lilith (Mamie Van Doren) is jealous of Roxana (Rhonda Fleming), the Western woman enslaved by Barbary pirates and rescued by Starbuck (Jeff Chandler). 1954, Universal Pictures Company, Inc.

Luck runs out when the ship is attacked by Barbary pirates who kill the father and abduct Roxana to sell on the Moroccan slave market.

Starbuck learns about her fate and collects his wager by being booked on a passage to France, where he sails to Morocco. He ingratiates himself to the sultan (Lee J. Cobb) because of his shooting prowess. The sultan appoints him as a rifle instructor to his infantrymen. Starbuck adopts Islamic customs and becomes a character in one of his exotic books.

The rest of the movie shows Starbuck living as a Moor, making plans to rescue Roxana and fighting the forces of an ambitious warlord. It ends with the Yankee returning to sea with his woman and the sultan presenting a scatterbrained blonde slave to an unsuccessful underling. Royal laughs seal the treaty.

Jeff Chandler shows why he was a first-rate action hero with this movie, one of the many costume dramas he made for U.I. He is a hero without special effects or outlandish gimmicks, an old-fashioned moun-

Mamie Van Doren plays Lillith, a sultry and scatterbrained harem girl in *Yankee Pasha*, filmed in Panavision. 1954, Universal Pictures Company, Inc.

tain man whose code of honor is matched by flawless gamesmanship. He is graceful when he performs his Islamic salutations, respectful in declining the services of a pliant slave and precise and dominant in winning two key *mano o mano* matches with the villain. His shooting contest in the forest and death fight over The Hooks is the one-two combo that takes down the evil warlord, Omar Id-Din (Bart [Rex Reason] Roberts).

Starbuck's code of honor turns the disgraced Roxana into a power coquette. His love is roughhewn and shatters the pledge of genteel society, but it is genuine and fails to acknowledge defeat. Because of Starbuck, Roxana rises from subversion and humiliation and ascends to the rank of lady again.

Rhonda Fleming is gorgeous as Roxana, the international prize. She is a New World woman returned to an old world way of life. Her attempt to rise above her social standing by teaching her fiancé a lesson in humility backfires when it is considered infidelity and duplicity. She is forced to flee America with her father to escape malicious gossip; her real punishment is enslavement in a mid-eastern harem.

She is the crown jewel of the slave vender's lot and causes battle between east and west. The redheaded firebrand is a rebel in the harem. Her co-prisoners are several Miss Universe contestants of 1954. They are honored to be the prizes of Omar Id-Din, but Roxana is full of power and defiance. This amuses the harem women, who think that she should just give in with a smile.

The sultan (Lee J. Cobb) presents Lilith (Mamie Van Doren) to Hassan Sendar (Hal March) as a dubious punishment for letting Starbuck escape.
1954, Universal Pictures Company, Inc.

The harem is an all-girls club at the beck-and-call of a salacious male ruler. The women ridicule the New World prize about monogamy, reflecting the philosophy of the patriarchal ruling class. A balance between male and female is not what the concubines approve of.

The idea of conversation between monogamous spouses befuddles one woman (Lisa Gaye). Conversation is useless to a harem girl because love is all that matters. She says, "When all is said of this (love), what is there to talk about?"

Bart Roberts—the future Rex Reason—makes for a convincing villain, Omar Id-Din. He speaks with the eloquence of exotic storybook villains. Some of his lines are: "A tasty morsel should always be well served" and "She is like the wild falcon whom I shall train to sit at my right hand."

Omar-Id-Din possesses a serious demeanor, perfect diction, excellent posture and good riding skills. He is fearless and brave and willing to face off with the western interloper at a moment's notice. His contempt for Starbuck is evident from the start when he refers to the westerner as "Infidel." The warlord's pride and breeding blind him to the westerner's simple strategy: to bait him and trap him using his own methods. This happens so many times that Bart winds up on The Hooks.

Hal March plays Hassan Sendar, a good-natured lieutenant who appreciates the westerner's tutelage in marksmanship. His main difference with Starbuck is about the treatment of women. To him, they are slaves tempered by a whip of convenience. Later, Starbuck admits to Roxana that, "In America, men are slaves to women" as their freedom ship sails home against a burnished sunset.

Mamie plays Lilith, a fair-skinned blonde harem girl in *Yankee Pasha*. She is chatty and bothersome, also defensive and disruptive. Her slave refrain is, "All my days, I will make offerings to my sovereign for having presented me to a master such as you." Her big scenes are a knockdown, drag-out fight with Roxana in the boudoir and a horseback riding bait-and-switch scheme that helps to bluff Omar Ib-Din at the outset of the last set-up. Wedded bliss to Lillith is Hassan Sendar's punishment for helping the westerner procure Roxana and escape to America. It is a commuted sentence, the sultan's last laugh.

Lee J. Cobb is gruff as the sultan; Benny Rubin is charming as Starbuck's blustered servant; and Philip Van Zandt is sneaky as the slave merchant. The Miss Universe contestants of 1954 play his white sale.

Francis Joins the WACS

Francis Joins the WACS: (1954-Universal-International-95 min.)
Lt. Peter Stirling: Donald O'Connor. *Capt. Jane Parker:* Julia (Julie) Adams. *Francis' Voice/ Gen. Kaye:* Chill Wills. *Cpl. Bunk Hilstrom:* Mamie Van Doren. *Maj. Louis Simpson:* Lynn Bari. *Lt. Valerie Humpert:* ZaSu Pitts. *Kate:* Mara Corday. *Lt. Dickson:* Allison Hayes,. *Sgt. Kipp:* Joan Shawlee. *Director:* Arthur Lubin. *Screenplay:* Devery Freeman and James B. Allardice. *Additional Dialogue:* Dorothy Reid (Dorothy Davenport). *Character created by:* David Stern. *Producer:* Ted Richmond. *Music:* Irving Gertz and Henry Mancini. *"Song of the Women's Army Corp":* Camilla Mays Frank. *Cinematography:* Irving Glassberg. *Editors:* Ted J. Kent and Russell F. Schoengarth.

Laughs were the order of the day with the Francis the Talking Mule series. *Francis* made its debut in 1947 and quickly established itself as a big moneymaker for the studio. Six more films followed and they took the mule and his human sidekick to places like the races, West Point, the Navy and the WACS.

For six of the films, Donald O'Connor starred as his sidekick. Mickey Rooney took over the role in the last film, *Francis in the Haunted House.* Chill Wills, the gravel-throated actor, supplied the voice of Francis in all of the movies except the last and was the chief reason for the character's appeal.

It is 1954 and The Pentagon is the heart and nerve center of the USA's national defense. It has entered the machine age and uses comput-

Peter Stirling (Donald O'Connor) and Francis, the Talking Mule, try to change the course of the war games in favor of the men. 1954, Universal Pictures Company, Inc.

Lt. Humpert (ZaSu Pitts) and Capt. Parker (Julia Adams) try to get a piece of Lt. Stirling (Donald O'Connor). 1954, Universal Pictures Company, Inc.

Francis Joins the WACS   87

Bunky Hilstrom (Mamie Van Doren) and Lt. Stirling (Donald O'Connor) cavort during maneuvers. 1954, Universal Pictures Company, Inc.

ers to classify, de-classify and re-classify officers. This comes in handy when it comes to selecting retreads for active duty.

Through an administrative snafu, Peter Stirling (Donald O'Connor) becomes a retread in the military when he is re-drafted and sent to serve at a WACS base. Before long, he is joined by his sidekick, Francis, the Talking Mule, who is there as a medical test subject. Laughs are encouraged by slapstick gags and the incongruity of a male WAC surrounded by women.

Captain Jane Parker (Julia Adams) resents being treated as a joke and thinks of women in the Army as serious business. Because the male ego finds it difficult to consider women other than kitchen maids or arm adornments, the captain sees a challenge to having him around as a social experiment. It becomes a battle of the sexes, not only in the outfit, but on the battalion level because of a camouflage contest between the Army and the WACS.

Lt. Stirling is reluctantly accepted by the female corps. Their reactions range from frustration to condescension. They plan to show him a thing or two because of his patronizing attitude. The movie ends with

Lynn Bari, Joan Shawlee, Mara Corday and Mamie Van Doren strike a pose. 1954, Universal Pictures Company, Inc.

the WACS being victorious and Francis is glad that he, too, joined the WACS.

The Francis factor in this movie is that he sounds exactly like General Kaye. That is because he is played by Chill Wills and this is the basis for a couple of bits where Francis gives absurd commands for soldiers to follow during the exercise. He also uses it to confound the WACS and has a nice routine with veteran comic ZaSu Pitts, who plays a nurse.

Francis Joins the WACS is the fifth film in the series. Francis and O'C were going through the motions by now and the only thing that saves this movie is the other performers. Julia Adams is wonderful as the flustered captain who masterminds a plan to show Lt. Stirling and General Kaye that the WACS can handle their share of the military payload.

Mamie Van Doren plays Corporal Bunky Hilstrom with a light comedic touch. Corporal Hilstrom is a cog in the wheel, a desk jockey that keeps the paperwork flowing and the laughs even-keeled with her wide-eyed innocence.

Chill Wills is the garrulous general who is confused when confronted with reports of a talking mule that sounds like him. ZaSu Pitts has a turn as a ditzy nurse who becomes further confused by Francis' jests in the name of the general. Jane Shawlee plays an officer with Mara Corday and Allison Hayes adding more sex appeal to the platoon.

The Second Greatest Sex

The Second Greatest Sex: (1955 - Universal-International - 82 min.-C)
Liza McClure: Jeanne Crain. *Matt Davis:* George Nader. *Katy Connors*: Kitty Kallen. *Job McClure:* Bert Lahr. *Birdie Snyder:* Mamie Van Doren. *Rev. Maxwell:* Keith Andes. *Tilda Bean*: Kathleen Case. *Roscoe Dobbs:* Paul Gilbert. *Alf Connors:* Tommy Rall. *Cassie Slater*: Edna Skinner. *Newt McClure:* Jimmy Boyd. *Director:* George Marshall. *Screenplay*: Charles Hoffman, *based on Lysistrata by* Aristophanes. *Producer:* Albert J. Cohen. *Music:* Henry Mancini. *Title Song by:* Ray Evans and Phil Moody. *Cinematography:* Wilfred M. Cline. *Editing:* Frank Gross.

    U-I was a maker of popular programmers so it was understandable that they patterned many of their scripts after other successful premises. One genre was the rural musical. *Oklahoma!* and *Seven Brides for Seven Brothers* were immensely popular and the theme was a surefire winner for the movies.
    To boost the concept, the producers resorted to a Greek tragedy to supply the outline. The premise to the movie is simple: take *Lysistrata,* transplant it to the American West and add show tunes and you have *The Second Greatest Sex.*
    In Osawkie, Kansas, the lamentation and wailing is over the absence of the men because of an intra-county war. The main combatants are the Osawkie men and their rivals from Mandaroon in a struggle over a safe that holds the deeds, contracts and entitlements that would give the owning town a seat of power recognized by Washington.

Matt Davis (George Nader) listens to fatherly advice from Job McClure (Bert Lahr) while the Reverend (Keith Andes) and McClure's son (Jimmy Boyd) look on. 1955, Universal Pictures Company, Inc.

Ambushes and fist fights make the country rumbles a crisis for the women. They are despondent without their men and sing worshipful songs lamenting their absence. The men folk's inability to come to a truce provokes a rebellion among the women. They withhold their love and ignore the men until it becomes apparent who the second greatest sex is.

Matt Davis (George Nader) is the town leader who plots for the power spot in Washington. The men folk blindly follow him and the battles rage until the women decide to have a war of their own. Liza McClure (Jeanne Crain) marries Matt Davis, but the honeymoon is anything but sweet and romantic. A strike occurs to protest the county wars and the men's will to power.

Music soothes the ruffled feathers and makes things palatable.

The Second Greatest Sex is mostly lachrymose and dull, with a few good moments, a couple of funny jokes, an occasional interesting dance number and catchy tune. It is lumbering, but has its bright spots.

Matt Davis (George Nader) courts Liza McClure (Jeanne Crain) with a robust tune. 1955, Universal Pictures Company, Inc.

Roscoe Dobbs (Paul Gilbert) is a traveling salesman who tries to rile the town's women with his wares. 1955, Universal Pictures Company, Inc.

Matt Davis (George Nader) and Liza McClure (Jeanne Crain) celebrate their wedding with a song and a dance number. 1955, Universal Pictures Company, Inc.

Jeanne Crain is beautiful but non-descript. She thinks out her part but still exudes more emotion than her co-star, George Nader. He never exuded much charisma but was still a likeable actor. Kathleen Case shows more life than the leads combined.

Bert Lahr deserves a lot of credit for his role as Job McClure, the befuddled family patriarch. He is funny and plays the part without effort. He is an old pro and rises above the material, squeezing his part for laughs. The only drawback is that, at times, he is almost cancelled out by Jimmy Boyd, an annoying adenoidal adolescent actor who plays his son. Newt grates on the nerves as soon as he speaks his first lines.

Keith Andes and Mamie Van Doren are wasted in small parts as an earnest square-jawed parson who sparks the love bug in the town's blonde maiden. They should have played the leads. There would have been more passion.

The soundtrack consists of seven songs that tell the story by themselves and make for an entertaining and campy combination of styles and moods. "What Good is a Woman Without a Man?" is the opening number and it is as infectious as it is imbecilic. A good old-fashioned frontier adulation of the men folk is the town's ladies social contract.

"Send Us a Miracle" is a weird ballet by Tommy Rall. It is a dream sequence hallucinated by Kathleen Case after she inhales the fumes of a traveling man's all-purpose cleaning elixir. Rall pulls out all stops with mid-air pirouettes and chandelier antics. Blue cowboy boots give his dancing an extra kick and the dazzling footwork gives Case something to hallucinate about. It is something you would expect in a musical western based on *Lysistrata*.

"Travellin' Man" is the snake oil dealer's chance to step out. He does his number to impress the town's spinster, whom he tries to loosen up with his brew. It gives her enough of a jolt to bounce around the set in a tease-and-come-hither routine with the huckster. "My Love is Yours" is a wedding proposal where Matt and Liza give it their all and fail to gild their frosted breath. "There's Gonna Be A Wedding" is a public announcement of their wedding. It is a big production number that is the calm before the storm. An interrupted honeymoon is the abstinent rupture that starts the revolution. "Lysistrata" is a hoedown stampede as the women assert their independence by recognizing Liza as their leader. With lyric rhymes like "Lysistrata-strata/Gotta,' Gotta'Gotta'" as the rallying cry, it leaves a lot to be desired, but the hoedown steps make up for it. "The Second Greatest Sex" is a *mea culpa* in this musical wrestling match. The men admit to being what they sing about as the women declare victory. What was once a Greek tragedy becomes a musical home on the range soap opera on the U.I. back lot.

Ain't Misbehavin'

Ain't Misbehavin': (1955-Universal-International- 83 min.-C)
Kenneth Post: Rory Calhoun. *Sarah Bernhardt Hatfield:* Piper Laurie. *Hal North:* Jack Carson. *Jackie:* Mamie Van Doren. *Anatole Piermont Rogers:* Reginald Gardiner. *Pat Beaton:* Barbara Britton. *Millie:* Dani Crayne. *Andy, Greek fisherman:* Peter Mamakos. *Director:* Edward Buzzell. *Producer:* Samuel Marx. *Screenplay:* Edward Buzzell. *Story:* Robert Carson. *Cinematography:* Wilfred M. Cline. *Music:* Henry Mancini and Frank Skinner. *Editor:* Paul Weatherwax.

Screwball comedic plots leavened with songs never hurt a movie, especially if they were in CinemaScope and had likable stars and good tunes. In *Ain't Misbehavin'*, the mixing of social classes causes love and friction for Kenneth Post III (Rory Calhoun), a third-generation Nob Hill scion, and Sarah Hatfield (Piper Laurie), a down-to-earth showgirl.

The Posts made their original fortune in banking. The power of finance produced an enterprise that includes electronics, mining, lumber, petroleum and steel. The third Kenneth Post is the 20th-century captain of industry. His favorite assets are yacht clubs, polo ponies, racing cars and ringside seats at popular nightclubs. Despite his passion for pleasure, Post enlarges the family empire.

They are married after a short but colorful courtship. What follows is the conflict supplied by Hal (Jack Carson), Post's business manager, and the bluebloods of Nob Hill. The chief antagonist is Pat Beaton

Jackie (Mamie Van Doren) gives the girls some advice on marrying rich while slipping into a silk stocking. 1955, Universal Pictures Company, Inc.

(Barbara Britton), Post's childhood friend. She had hoped to become Mrs. Kenneth Post III and the rebuff for a commoner has set her mind to scheming.

A series of staged public embarrassments for Sarah finds a cover in Hal's suggestion that she becomes a lady of refinement. A series of mishaps and misunderstandings separates the couple before they face the music at The Rowdy Club with a closing of hugs and kisses.

Ain't Misbehavin' is a likeable urbane screwball musical. Class conflict has always been a reliable staple of musical comedies. Some of the best bits are when Sarah Hatfield perplexes the bluebloods with her off-the-cuff humor. They don't know if she is serious or facetious.

The games of the rich and powerful are contrasted with the schemes of the working-class showgirls. Sarah is no different than the other chorines because the first thing she smells is Post's fortune after Hal invites her to have dinner with the businessman. Love cancels out her original intentions.

Rory Calhoun is the perfect as the Howard Hughes-type captain of industry. His rugged outdoorsman type looks good in a suit and he handles

Ain't Misbehavin' 99

Mamie Van Doren (l) and Piper Laurie (r) vie for the attention and bank assets of Rory Calhoun. 1955, Universal Pictures Company, Inc.

Mamie Van Doren shows why she should have been the movie's star in the film's opening Mambo sequence. 1955, Universal Pictures Company, Inc.

Piper Laurie sizzles in a production number. 1955, Universal Pictures Company, Inc.

boardrooms and dance floors with a sophistication that adds dimension to the character.

Calhoun plays the straight man well, caught between the Sarah's addled love and Hal's intrusive meddling. He is a fool because of love and it fits well into their rollercoaster romance. He is almost a stooge without a clue although he goes with his heart and that's why he winds up with Sarah.

Piper Laurie is vivacious and sensual as Sarah Bernhardt Hatfield. She makes a poor first impression, coming off as a single-minded hustler and not ashamed to admit it. The hard-bitten sarcasm is a stark contrast to her real personality.

She is a girl from the old neighborhood, one who knows how to keep score and catch peanuts at the ballgame, shuck oysters and drink champagne on a fishing boat and dance like a temptress who can turn black and white into color.

It is her down-to-earth humor that grounds the careless flyer after he was sent up because of her dancing charms. Piper Laurie is enchanting when she sings her songs and performs her dances. At a party, she shakes a jigger in a gold lame dress and it is every man for himself. Laurie displays good comic timing, too.

Jack Carson had the conniving buddy routine down pat for so long that he need only waltz though it for this movie. He is funny because his anxiety is the fodder for many of the comic bits. He frets and disrupts while playing the innocent. His aim is obvious, to separate Sarah from Post's fortune.

Hal is Shakespeare's Iago blended with a mother hen. He is Post's major domo and board of directors' eyes and ears, a public relations man who is a shadow that frames the picture. His scheming is what sets the pace for the story.

Reginald Gardiner is excellent as Uncle Pierpont. He is always drunk and on the lookout for new things of interest. He is mesmerized by Sarah when he meets his nephew's new bride at the coming-out party.

Mamie and Dani Crayne play Sarah's showgirl roommates, Jackie and Millie. Millie is the level-headed member of the trio. She sings, dances and stays in the background. The same cannot be said for Jackie. She is so illuminating that she outshines everyone when she is on the screen.

Mamie shares dance time with Piper Laurie and Dani Crayne in a nightclub Mambo number that is televised by an invention viewed by the rich leading man at the beginning of the movie. There is also a rousing impromptu song-and-dance sequence at the Posts' wedding reception.

The story may be about the romance between the leads, but it is Mamie Van Doren who captivates the ayes with sensuous teases. Jackie is the ultimate chorine and has the appropriate philosophy to prove it. "That's the work it works!" is how she sums up the male/female dichotomy and the rites of passion. She applies that philosophy to how to snag a rich husband.

Whenever Mamie is in a scene, she takes over until it becomes apparent that she should have starred as the lead, Sarah Bernhardt Hatfield. It is a realization that could ruin the movie if the viewer dwells on it too long. If she was cast in the lead, *Ain't Misbehavin'* would have ranked with the 1950s' best gold-digger movies. The casting choice is so obvious and to not see it is ironic for a studio that signed Mamie as serious competition to Marilyn Monroe's claim to queen of the blondes.

The movie's shooting title was *Third Girl to the Left*.

Running Wild

Running Wild: *aka* The Girl in the Cage (USA) (1955-Universal-International-81 min.)
Ralph Barclay: William Campbell. *Irma Bean:* Mamie Van Doren. *Ken Osanger:* Keenan Wynn. *Scotty Cluett:* Jan Merlin. *Leta Novak*: Kathleen Case. *Vince Pomeroy*: John Saxon. *Lt. Newpole*: Walter Coy. *Osanger's Mother*: Grace Mills. *Director:* Abner Biberman. *Producer*: Howard Pine. *Screenplay*: Leo Townsend. *Novel:* Ben Benson. *Cinematography*: Ellis W. Carter. *Editors*: Edward Curtiss and Ray Snyder. *Music:* Joseph Gershenson.

U-I excelled at making fast-moving crime dramas that clocked in on the short side. They may be considered inconsequential to purists and of no relative worth to the serious collectors, but they earned their entertainment value because of unique touches.

It could be a faded star giving an earnest performance or a one-shot newcomer in a quickie showcase made to test audience reaction. Maybe it was because it was a minor film made by a director of better known movies or it had familiar character actors doing quirky bits.

Running Wild was one of these gritty movies, an Arthurian drama with a rock 'n' roll soul. It's Hot Rod versus Scotty in a battle to bring down the Boss and free Anita, the kept maiden from behind the Iron Curtain.

The movie was directed by Abner Biberman, a character actor from the Thirties and Forties who had the distinction of being the director of oddball dramas for Universal-International in the Fifties. He would later

Title card for *Running Wild*, one of the early rock and roll movies. 1955, Universal Pictures Company, Inc.

Tough guy (William Campbell) and oppressed hard luck girl (Kathleen Case) bond in a tender moment. 1955, Universal Pictures Company, Inc.

direct intense character studies like *The Looters* ('55), *The Night Runner* ('57) and *Floodtide* ('58) for U-I.

Running Wild is a rambunctious chop-shop drama with rock 'n' roll licks. The hero is a cop (William Campbell) acting like a hotrod punk by the name of Ralph Barclay. Barclay has a greasy pompadour and a perpetual smirk on his face. His pose is that of a gunslinger, always ready for a split-second showdown.

The chop-shop boss is Ken Osanger (Keenan Wynn), a corrupt oldster who hangs out with the kids at the edge of town in a malt shop called the Cove. Scotty Cluett (Jan Merlin) is Osanger's foreman. Cluett is the Midwestern farm boy gone bad. He takes an instant disliking to Barclay the moment he is hired by Osanger, who enjoys the tension because it keeps both men sharp.

The ice pick that chips away at the men is Cluett's girlfriend, Irma Bean (Mamie Van Doren). She is a jitterbugging tease who sets up Barclay for beatings by Cluett because of her flirting. Barclay is also nagged by Osanger's use of a kept brunette (Kathleen Case) whom he uses as a means to infiltrate the tough guy's confidence.

Barclay falls in love with the brunette once he understands the circumstances of her bondage. He busts the carjacking ring in spite of himself. Love wins in the end, but it is tested by a wheelchair and Cold War immigration policies.

Abner Biberman has directed a tight action movie. The characters have enough angles to them to make them interesting. The smalltime air to the operation makes it a study in small-town corruption. Osanger is a low-rent crime boss who plays it as a populist; he even works at his own gas station. The farm is

Irma Bean (Mamie Van Doren) poses with her best friend, a juke box. 1955, Universal Pictures Company, Inc.

another matter. That is where his mother runs things and the lowdown of the hijacking and chop-shop setup gets planned and ironed out.

William Campbell is one of the many faceless hotrod punks who played the leads in obscure crime dramas. The movies were usually the products of skid-row productions, unlike *Running Wild,* one of many Universal-International's quickie crime capers.

Campbell plays it tough enough to fool Osanger, but Scotty Cluett is another matter. Jan Merlin's smirk makes him look like The Joker and

Second-tier thug Scotty Cluett (Jan Merlin) with his hot rod moll, Irma Bean (Mamie Van Doren). 1955, Universal Pictures Company, Inc.

William Campbell strikes his best tough guy pose to impress Kathleen Case. 1955, Universal Pictures Company, Inc.

he never fails to humiliate Barclay at every turn. William Campbell and Jan Merlin make good enemies because they were third-level tough guys, a pleasant element of cheap, oddball dramas.

Mamie is coquettish as Merlin's girlfriend. She gets to entice Campbell, but backs off in time for Merlin to become confrontational. Van Doren's jibes and jitterbugging are explosive; so is Keenan Wynn's temper.

Wynn plays a role that he would for most of his career: the blustery no-nonsense blowhard boss. His style gets things done until he becomes undone by the cop posing as the mechanic. The sensitivity award goes to Kathleen Case as Lita. She is a kept woman who has sacrificed her public respect with a private pride that has provided freedom for a loved one. John Saxon has a small role as the gang member who tries to go straight. He doesn't buy the farm but, in a way, he does because it is his last stop.

Star In the Dust

Star In the Dust: aka Law Man (USA) (1956-Universal-International-80 min.-C)
Sheriff Bill Jorden: John Agar. *Ellen Ballard:* Mamie Van Doren. *Sam Hall:* Richard Boone. *Nellie Mason:* Coleen Gray. *George Ballard:* Leif Erickson. *Orval Jones:* James Gleason. *Mike MacNamara :*Paul Fix. *Nan Hogan:* Randy Stuart. *Lew Hogan:* Harry Morgan. *The Music Man:* Terry Gilkyson. *Director:* Charles F. Haas. *Producer:* Albert J. Zugsmith. *Screenplay:* Oscar Brodney. *Novel:* Lee Leighton. *Cinematography:* John L. Russell. *Music:* Frank Skinner. *Song:* "Sam Hill": Terry Gilkyson. *Editor:* Ray Snyder.

Star In the Dust is an eccentric western that is uneven in its tone and execution. Sometimes it works to the viewer's advantage and there are times when it stumbles. Part of the movie's strangeness comes from the weird performance by Richard Boone as Sam Hall, the imprisoned villainous hired gun who awaits execution. The other is the intriguing and ultimately unsettling guitar-playing troubadour who narrates the action through song.

Sam Hall is the lynch pin in the range war between the cattlemen and the ranchers. He is guilty of murdering three ranchers and it is the sentiment that he was hired by George Ballard (Leif Erickson), a wealthy and powerful land baron.

Sheriff Borden (John Agar) is the son of a legend and his task to oversee the hanging of the noxious outlaw. The townspeople want to

Title card for *Star in the Dust*, a revenge western. 1956, Universal Pictures Company, Inc.

hang the man but the lawman follows the law to its final letter at six o'clock-hanging time. The tension mounts as tempers flare during the day.

The sheriff loves Ellen Ballard (Mamie), the villain's sister. The farmers feel that it has prejudiced him against them. He claims partiality and it is not until the end that sides are delineated and the outlaw meets his reward.

John Agar gives an earnest performance as the beleaguered sheriff who shoulders two burdens. He is the son of a legend and he has to stem the fury of frontier justice. The sheriff has his hands full with carrying out the letter of the law. The town wants to lynch Hall because they know that the cattlemen are going to rescue him. His predicament is viewed as weakness by the other players in the game.

The businessmen look at the sheriff as being weak tea compared to his heroic father. There is even a betting pool with 8:3 odds that Hall will escape. The school teacher wants to take advantage of the sheriff's disadvantage by leading the farmers in a revolt that will make him the town leader. The spinster thumbs her nose at propriety by flaunting her affair with the bad man and using incriminating letters to ensure his bust out. A rancher's wife is led to believe that her husband was responsible for

Lucy Ballard (Mamie Van Doren) seeks reassurance from her brother (Leif Ericson) that he is not the evil force behind the violent land grabs that have started a range war. 1956, Universal Pictures Company, Inc.

Sam Hall (Richard Boone) is kept in check by the sheriff (John Agar) as Orval Jones (James Gleason) looks on in admiration. 1956, Universal Pictures Company, Inc.

A montage of pivotal scenes from *Star in the Dust*. 1957, Illus. Film-Buhne.

hiring the gun man and aids in a failed escape attempt.

His success is assured by Ellen Ballard's decision about forked intentions. Mamie's last role for U.I. is a stark departure from her dumb blonde parts for the studio. Ellen Ballard is forceful and independent, a character caught in a dilemma caused by blood. Her love for her brother and the sheriff are put to the test at the end when the ranchers and cattlemen clash. In the chaos, she chooses the reform that comes with new love.

Leif Erickson has his day in the sun before he finds out what it's like to be cut down to size by his kid sister. Erickson growls his part with a tiger's rasp and a predatory gaze. He is in total control until the end when he goes out in a blaze. It is a vengeful rancher that shoots him when it comes to light that the farmers were not trespassing on ranch land when they were murdered. Hall killed him for the one-thousand-dollar-per-head bounty. The shot that fells Ballard also sends Hall off to a mid-air farewell.

Richard Boone plays Hall with such a self-assured air that the viewer almost expects him to get away with the murders. He mesmerizes the town spinster (Coleen Gray), pushes the grizzly newly appointed deputy (James Gleason) over the edge and almost makes a smooth getaway. It's mostly the heroic ballad that gives Hall a sense of indestructibility. The rest is Boone's forceful characterization.

Paul Fix is a wise deputy who waxes philosophical about the unsettling day. He compares the atmosphere in the town with the period before a cyclone hits: "...a feeling of emptiness, like the air had been sucked out of space."

Harry Morgan plays an angry rancher and Randy Stuart plays his wife, a prairie woman who once had an affair with George Ballard. Coleen Gray plays the spinster as a victim of a repressed upbringing. James Gleason dusted off his grizzled vet style for a jack-of-all trades who becomes a hero.

Although Terry Gilkyson's guitar score and lyrical lament occasionally grate on the nerves, it is the sparse music that gives *Star in the Dust* its unique atmosphere. It is the perfect accompaniment to a story that starts as a slow simmer and ends with a rolling boil. The lack of orchestral arrangements is also true to the prairie locale, where the natural elements like the setting sun or the cool evening shade have as much personality as the characters.

The writing is deceptively simple, but Oscar Brodney deserves credit for building the tension in such a credible manner that you don't realize all of the film's elements are going to come to a head in the final shootout. It is the banality of evil rising to the surface done in the manner of a western tragedy. The action also takes place within the timeframe of one day. He also loads his script with snappy dialogue and memorable lines.

Charles Haas has a straightforward directing style, one that is suitable to the matter-of-fact principle of the script. It is the beginning of an association with Albert Zugsmith that would continue at MGM. Even under the U-I logo, Albert Zugsmith lent his weirdness to the productions. *Star in the Dust* is no exception. Leave it to Zugsmith to take a revenge drama and turn it into a tortured western where the acoustic guitar score chokes on the dust that swirls beneath a hanging man's feet.

The Girl In Black Stockings

The Girl In Black Stockings: aka Black Stockings or Wanton Murder (USA) (1957-Warner Bros.-73 min.) *David Hewson*: Lex Barker. *Beth Dixon*: Anne Bancroft. *Harriet Ames*: Mamie Van Doren. *Edmund Parry*: Ron Randell. *Julia Parry*: Marie Windsor. *Sheriff Jess Holmes*: John Dehner. *Norman Grant*: John Holland. *Louise Miles*: Diana Vandervlis. *Dr. John Aitkin:* Richard Cutting. *Indian Joe*: Larry Chance. *Frankie Pierce*: Gerald Frank. *Bartender*: Dan Blocker. *Director*: Howard W. Koch. *Producer*: Aubrey Schenk. *Screenplay*: John C. Higgins. *Story*: Stephen Longstreet. *Cinematography*: Carl Guthrie. *Editor:* John Schreyer. *Score*: Les Baxter.

David Hewson (Lex Barker) is a Los Angeles lawyer who takes a drive to anywhere and winds up at Parry Lodge, a Utah vacation resort where singles commingle and some brass rings turn into gold. One night, the party atmosphere of a lakeside dance is ruined by the discovery of a dead woman in the woods. The coroner notes the savagery of the crime and suggests that it may be the start of a pattern. It is.

The murders are a challenge for Sheriff Holmes (John Dehner), the small-town lawman with the big-city mind. He is aloof and calculating, sizing up the suspects with a wry wit. Nothing perturbs him as he investigates the murders by getting under the skin of his suspects.

Hewson is a tough guy with a decisive attitude. He considers himself above suspicion and often collides with the sheriff during the investigation. His main concern is Beth Dixon (Anne Bancroft), a caretaker whose quiet soul and calm exterior harbor a dark personality.

Title lobby card for *The Girl In Black Stockings*. 1957, United Artists Corp.

Beth is a startling contradiction to the couple she serves: Edmund Parry (Ron Randell), a bitter misogynist paraplegic, and his doting sister, Julia (Marie Windsor). Edmond and Julia are the strange siblings that run the resort in a town that their ancestors helped to settle.

Other suspects are Frankie (Gerald Frank), the lumberyard Lothario, and Louise Miles (Diana Vandervlis), a prim and man hungry Nordic ice queen. The sheriff also keeps an eye on Norman Grant (John Holland), a washed-up screen actor and his faithful groupie, Harriet Ames (Mamie Van Doren). They are guests at the resort because Grant needs to regain his vigor as he studies a rare script that may result in a comeback to films.

The Girl in Black Stockings has a creepy feeling to it because of the tortured characters. Their self-hatred poisons the mountain vacation spot just as much as the series of mutilation murders. The film is less a murder mystery than it is a character study of tormented souls.

The lack of pulse-quickening moments is curious considering the level of sadism present in the story. From the mutilation murders that are described in detail to a horrific lumberyard death, it is all done between sunlight and shadows.

Mamie Van Doren, Lex Barker, Anne Bancroft and Marie Windsor pose for a group portrait. 1957, United Artists Corp.

Lex Barker ably fills out the role of the soul-searching wanderer who becomes involved in a defining moment of his life. The drive to nowhere ends with the need to survive a psychopath on the loose. Barker is intrepid in competing with the sheriff to solve the murders and bring the killer to justice. In the end, he is cuckolded when he does corner the real killer. He is double-trumped when the sheriff emerges as the victor with another achievement to pin on his reputation.

A montage of suspicious characters from the movie. 1957, Illus. Film-Buhne.

Anne Bancroft gives a smooth-as-velvet performance as Beth Dixon, the altruistic caretaker. Bancroft had a torrid bobcat feline persona during her early years on the B-movie circuit. The '50s hold some of her best performances, although the *cineastes* and critics prefer to mention the Oscar- and Tony-winning roles, not to mention her iconic Mrs. Robinson. Beth Dixon turns out to be a kitten with a whip and not even former Tarzan Lex Barker saw it coming.

The strangest performances of the movie are provided by Ron Randell and Marie Windsor. They are self-loathing and parasitic, motivated by guilt, hate and a false sense of concern for others. Should it be a wonder that their lodge would be the setting for a series of gruesome murders?

Randell's performance is remarkable considering the complexity of his character and the limited space he has to express himself. Truly creepy and vitriolic, his spit is bile that covers the movie. Windsor appears to be a mannequin with lines. She could very well be the wind with napkins.

Mamie offers up her blonde bimbo image for sacrifice in a bit of tongue-in-cheek ghoulishness. Harriet Ames is an adoring fan of Norman Grant who once waited in the rain for his autograph. She is an airhead who strokes his ego and makes a nice pool accessory. She makes a drunken fool out of herself at a dinner party when she flirts with the bitter Edmond and teases him. Later, she suffers the razor's edge while rehearsing a scene with the pie-eyed actor.

Gerald Frank is the tough-guy lumberjack Lothario who makes a misstep at work one day and Larry Chance is chilling as Indian Joe, a ranch hand who confesses to a murder but was really working off a bad

Mamie poses for a bathing suit shot in a composite photo. 1957, Illus. Film-Buhne.

hangover with some big talk. Minor characters that add personality to the movie are a snap-happy crime photographer, a stern coroner, a seedy private eye and a sarcastic bartender.

Untamed Youth

Untamed Youth (1957-Warner Brothers-81 min.)
Penny Lowe: Mamie Van Doren. *Jane Lowe:* Lori Nelson. *Ross Tropp:* John Russell. *Bob Steele*: Don Burnett. *Judge Cecelia Steele Tropp*: Lurene Tuttle. *Jack Landis*: Glenn Dixon. *Baby*: Yvonne Lime. *Lillibet*: Jeanne Carmen. *Sheriff Mitch Bowers*: Robert Foulk. *Duke:* Wayne Taylor. *Ralph*: Jerry Barclay. *Pinky:* Wally Brown. *Director*: Howard W. Koch. *Producer*: Aubrey Schenck. *Screenplay*: John C. Higgins. *Story*: Stephen Longstreet. *Cinematography*: Carl E. Guthrie. *Original Music*: Les Baxter. *Songs*: Lenny Adelson, Jerry Capehart and Eddie Cochran.

Penny and Jane Lowe (Mamie Van Doren and Lori Nelson) are sisters who are sentenced to 30 days on a cotton and potato plantation after being convicted of hitchhiking and skinny-dipping. Judge Steele (Lurene Tuttle) uses her bench to send misdemeanors to the plantation once owned by her late husband. Boss Ross Tropp (John Russell) is now the cruel taskmaster who owns the farm, having bought it from the judge after they secretly wed.

It is a season of bumper crops ruined by lack of labor and many farmers reap a rotten harvest because they don't have ample workers. The secret to Boss Tropp's success is that he augments his indentured work force with illegal farm workers from south of the border. Secret deals and clandestine arrangements allow him to supply labor to neighboring planters who are financially pressed.

Tropp's growing empire is threatened when Bob Steele (Don

The Lowe Sisters (Lori Nelson and Mamie Van Doren) are caught skinny dipping by a shady sheriff. 1957, Illus. Film-Buhne.

Burnett), the judge's son, returns to town after his discharge from the Navy. The naïve judge arranges for her son to work on his former property for a man that he doesn't know is his stepfather. It is only a matter of time before he finds out that his birthright has been given away to a hustler and that his mother is a stranger caught up in a scheme that disgusts him.

He is enlightened by Jane Lowe, who is embittered by the crass corruption that permeates the work camp: sexual favors for indoor work, canned dog food in lieu of beef stew and overwork in the relentless heat. It is her persistence that brings down Tropp and uncovers his impressive set-up. In the film's climax, he is busted in the middle of a shady deal to import three hundred illegal workers for his business.

The ads for *Untamed Youth* herald Mamie Van Doren as "The Girl Built Like a Platinum Powerhouse." The movie was condemned by the Legion of Decency, but still made an impressive profit for the studio. It is a camp delight but it is also a brutal movie. Sadism swelters in the cotton fields beneath the sun and the inmates are the rock 'n' roll generation at the mercy of the Old South migrated to Southern California. Boss Tropp is the big daddy who tames the misdemeanors and the babes who wind up on his work farm.

The subplots of illegal immigration and undocumented farm workers still have resonance today. Abuse of power never fades from municipal view and sex as a weapon is cruelly displayed by the doomed love affair of

Boss Tropp (John Russell) looks over the new recruits for his plantation.
1957, Warner Bros. Pict. Corp.

Penny Lowe heats up the mess hall jamboree with her side kicks.
1957, Warner Bros. Pict. Corp.

the duped judge and the plights of some of the female inmates. Rock 'n' roll or "African antics," as Pinky the cook calls it, is the music that sanitizes the incarceration. It's either dancing at the mess hall or in the cotton fields.

Untamed Youth has the same dark look to it that Howard W. Koch's other Mamie Van Doren movies have. There is something oppressive about the cinematography. Things seem too close for comfort, even in the outdoors. The claustrophobia adds to the unpleasant atmosphere of the movie.

The only light is at the end when Mamie stars in a television production number, "Go, Go Calypso." It is an upbeat ending to a grim film. Still, the harvester rolls along while Don and Jane, newlyweds, visit their plantation. Ma Steele - the former judge - sits at home and now serves as the Steele matriarch.

Mamie plays a good girl in a bad way. For her, Southern California comfort is a hell made of cotton. Her ambition is to make it big as a singer in Los Angeles, singing four songs along the way. She steams up the barracks with a song-and-dance tease and does a nice turn on the film's closing production number.

Lori Nelson is the movie's heroine, a tough-talking fighter who does not allow anyone to intimidate her. She criticizes Tropp to his face, chal-

Penny Lowe pulls out all the stops in a bid to maintain her independence in the barracks. 1957, Warner Bros. Pict. Corp.

Boss Tropp (John Russell) and Penny Lowe in a posed struggle.
1957, Warner Bros. Pict. Corp.

lenges Steele's manhood, lends guidance to her older sister and asserts herself among the other inmates with her fists.

Jane Lowe is put into a compromising situation with the iron-handed corrupt cowpoke and leads him on a chase that ends with his arrest. As an inmate on a corrupt cotton plantation, she disrupts the crooked power scheme, bringing down an evil rancher and canceling out an obliging magistrate. She nets the good guy and a marriage that makes her the new lady of the plantation.

John Russell is rough as the plantation owner. Nothing is out of the question or too low for him if it means increasing his power. His hold over the judge is sickening and makes him out as a gigolo turning a hustle with a confused and lonely old lady. He bought her judgeship and uses the power of the bench to change the laws that help him build his business.

Lurene Tuttle is hysterical as the judge who busts her hustler husband in a climatic ending. The judge is blinded by love and takes her ruination in stride when all is lost in the end. Her final judicial act is to pardon the inmates after she has Tropp arrested. She resigns from the bench and enjoys the company of Bob and his future bride, Jane.

Yvonne Lime plays Baby, a vulnerable teenager. She is the movie's sympathy card, a shy underage pregnant field worker. Her death starts the plot that brings Tropp down. Wally Brown, an old-time comedian, is fine as Pinky, the jive-talking sleazy pot-bellied cook. He is the one who suggests that Tropp check out Penny's musical talent. Eddie Cochran, the rock 'n' roll star, plays a singing cotton picker.

Mamie performs "Rolling Stone," "Oo-Ba-La-Baby," "Salamander" and "Go, Go Calypso." Eddie Cochran sings "Cotton Picker" under the midday sun.

Le Bellissime Gambe di Sabrina (The Beautiful Legs of Sabrina)

Le Bellissime Gambe di Sabrina
aka The Beautiful Legs of Sabrina (USA)
Madchen miit hubschen Beinen (West Germany)
(1958-Central Cinema-PGC Rome-109 min.)
Sabrina: Mamie Van Doren. *Teo:* Antonio Cifariello. *Toni:* Rossana Martini. *Mario:* Raffaele Pisu. *Il Commendatore:* Enrico Viarisio. *With:* Irene Aloisi, Mario Ambrosino, Willy Birgel and Lola Braccini. *Director:* Camillio Mastrocinque. *Screenplay:* Edoardo Anton and Marcello Fondato.

Le Bellissime Gambe di Sabrina is an Italian comedy about love, larceny and beautiful legs. Crime and mistaken identity are one and the same when positive identification is finding a pair of tattooed legs in a robbery photo. It is the only hope in solving the robbery of a Baden-baaden jewelry store.

Count Gaffredo (Raffaele Pisi) is fake royalty but a bona-fide international jewel thief. He keeps it in the family by using his niece Sabrina (Mamie Van Duren), a model, in his plans. Sabrina's legs become the only clue in a Baaden-baaden jewelry store robbery.

An unexpected link turns up in the work of Teo (Antonio Cifariello), a young photographer who is using up rolls to win a contest about launching a new brand of women's stockings. Teo's collection of leg photos includes a shot of a tattooed leg and he knows who it belongs to: Sabrina, a model who works at a fashion studio.

The discovery sets the stage for a romantic comedy about a thief's code, a lover's credo, and the shuffling of fates by an unseen hand. Teo's

Cover for the German press book of The Beautiful Legs of Sabrina. 1959, Illus. Film-Buhne. (Central Cinema-PGC Rome)

A montage of scenes from the film. 1959, Illus. Film-Buhne.
(Central Cinema-PGC Rome)

photo alarms the robbery gang and they plot to retrieve it at all costs. Mario (Raffaele Pisu) and Toni (Rossana Martini) spearhead the effort to get Teo's photo of Sabrina's legs.

Teo is the catalyst for the action. The camera that captured the tattooed leg also connects the film's points of reference. The photographer becomes obsessed with Sabrina's legs and wants to use them for an ad campaign for stockings.

The photographer and the model meet and fall in love during the hunt. A Vespi scooter provides the ride for Sabrina and Teo's passion. They cruise through Rome, frustrating the gang in their attempts to destroy the evidence. In the end, the gang's secret is safe as Sabrina gives up her life as a jewel thief because of love.

Le Bellissime Gambe di Sabrina is typical of postwar Italian comedies: breezy and cosmopolitan with the requisite sex appeal. Mamie and Antonio Cierforeeli perform well together, providing the necessary sparks and laughs. A droll pageant director and gregarious crime mastermind add to the comedic sparring. Legs are the lure but they are not really the beautiful legs of Sabrina. Mamie's legs did not conform to the Italian norm for gams and a double was used!

Another montage from the film. 1959, Illus. Film-Buhne.

Teacher's Pet

Teacher's Pet: (1958-Paramount-120 min.)
James Gannon/James Gallagher: Clark Gable. *Erica Stone:* Doris Day. *Dr. Hugo Pine:* Gig Young. *Peggy DeFore:* Mamie Van Doren. *Barney Kovac:* Nick Adams. *Harold Miller:* Peter Baldwin. *Katy Fuller:* Marion Ross. *Roy:* Charles Lane. *Guide:* Jack Albertson. *Mrs. Kovac:* Vivian Nathan. *Director:* George Seaton. *Screenplay:* Fay Kanin and Michael Kanin. *Cinematography:* Haskell Boggs. *Editor:* Alma Macrorie. *Music:* Roy Webb.

Hard liquor and chest-thumping arm wrestle with urbane wit and tempered charm when James Gannon (Clark Gable), the grizzled tough-guy editor of *The New York Evening Chronicle*, squares off with Erica Stone (Doris Day), a caring night school journalism instructor. It is a bout between the pig-iron typewriter and the birth of the new journalism as the street beat gets paved over by sensitive linguistics and fuzzy paradigms.

Gannon is miffed when his managing editor suggests that he accept the request to speak to Erica Stone's journalism night class. The seasoned vet believes that nuts-and-bolts journalism can only be learned through practical experience and to learn it the genteel way is to take away its edge.

To make a point, he enrolls as a student incognito and his expertise earns him the teacher's special attention. She believes that she has found a student with prodigious talent and encourages him. Gannon begins to feel guilty when he learns that his teacher's zeal is caused by her respect

132   The Films of Mamie Van Doren

Advertisment for *Teacher's Pet*. 1957, Perlsea Company and Paramount Pictures Corp.

for her father, a Pulitzer Prize-winner for his small-town newspaper. She is despondent when she learns that he is the city editor pulling her leg.

It is their respective chums that set up the motions for them to understand each other. The hard-nosed city editor learns the importance of sensitivity from Dr. Hugo Pine (Gig Young), a renowned psychiatrist with eclectic tastes. The journalism teacher learns about the power of rock 'n' roll from Peggy DeFore (Mamie Van Doren), a nightclub entertainer.

Teacher's Pet has a clever script that is brought out with verve by the leads and the supporting players. Clark Gable and Doris Day balance Gig Young and Mamie Van Doren.

A newsroom montage from *Teacher's Pet*. 1957, Perlsea Company and Paramount Pictures Corp.

Peggy DeFore is a nightclub singer in love with The King, Clark Gable. 1957, Perlsea Company and Paramount Pictures Corp.

Clark Gable is bluster and bravado with credentials from the old school of reporting. Gable creates a character that blends in well with the noisy newsroom and the press that rolls out the latest edition. He is proud of never having reached high school and being educated by the experience that translates into ink and newsprint.

Doris Day combines a mannerly sex appeal with a polished education. She is a dreamer and a charmer whose naïve optimism turns out to be more mean-tempered than Gable's gruff affronts. Brisk means nothing to her when she sizes up the editor through his girlfriend, Peggy DeFore, during her performance of "The Girl Who Invented Rock and Roll."

Gig Young is a highlight as the psychiatrist, raconteur, author and almost-perfect nice guy. It is easy to see why he earned a nomination for Best Supporting Actor. The good doctor aids Stone with his sound counseling. Pine is Gannon's means of becoming sensitive and understanding, the transformation of the Neanderthal Man into a kinder, gentler journalist—putty, instead of brick.

Mamie plays the chorus girl with the headline act. She sings and dances when not keeping Gable company. Rock 'n' roll is what separates her from the other chorines. Mamie sings her trademark song, "The Girl Who Invented Rock and Roll" and it puts a bump and a bustle in the professor's step. That is when Day takes the upper hand and wins the battle of wills with Gable. Along the way, in real life, she also trimmed a scene with Mamie and the King, and it remains on the cutting-room floor.

Nick Adams plays Gannon's protégée, Barney Kovac, the copy boy. Mrs. Kovac (Vivien Nathan) begs the editor to fire her boy so he can finish school. Gannon struggles because he wants the kid to be old school, but second guesses his nuts-and-bolts approach because of his encounter with Stone.

High School Confidential

High School Confidential: aka Young Hellions (reissue title-USA) (1958-MGM-85 min.)
Tony Baker: Russ Tamblyn. *Arlene Williams*: Jan Sterling. *J.I. Coleridge*: John Drew Barrymore. *Gwen Dulaine*: Mamie Van Doren. *Joan Staples*: Diane Jurgens. *Bix*: Ray Anthony. *Jerry Lee Lewis*: Himself. *Mr. A.*: Jackie Coogan. *Quinn:* Charles Chaplin, Jr. William Remington Kane: Lyle Talbot. Wheeler-Dealer: William Wellman, Jr. Steve Bentley: Michael Landon. With: Grabowski, Mel Welles and Texas Joe Foster. Director: Jack Arnold. Screenplay: Lewis Meltzer and Robert Blees (also the story).

High School Confidential is a good-natured exploitation movie posing as a social commentary on the crisis facing American teenagers. The topic is juvenile delinquency and the cause of the madness is drugs, chiefly marijuana, the devil's weed. The adult authorities do not want to hear about progressive social theories that mollycoddle teenagers. They are hardnosed and recognize the evils of drug use. To them, pot and heroin are the same thing: tools to destroy American youth.

The Devil's advocate is Tony Baker (Russ Tamblyn), an arrogant punk who plans to make a name for himself at his new high school. He has been in high school for seven years and none the wiser for it. He aims high and does not plan on getting there by climbing the ladder a rung at a time; a giant leap will do.

The local high school is the power station and a change in command is about to occur when Tony Baker, the wise-guy newcomer, challenges the

Suggestive ad for *High School Confidential*, produced by Albert J. Zugsmith. 1958, Loew's Inc.

High School Confidential 137

Cover for the German press book of High School Confidential.
1959, Film Neues Programm.

A posed shot of 50's decadence, courtesy of Mamie Van Doren and Russ Tamblyn. 1958, Loew's Inc.

supremacy of J.R. (John Drew Barrymore), the hotshot in charge. His aim is to become a big-league drug dealer and he plans to achieve that by taking over the Wheelers and Dealers, the high-school gang.

J.R. is not impressed by the inroads Baker has made with his flamboyant behavior; that includes losing his girlfriend (Diane Jurgens)

Diane Jurgens, Russ Tamblyn, Jan Sterling, John Drew Barrymore and Mamie Van Doren pose for the camera. 1958, Loew's Inc.

to the thug. She is a nice girl who grazes for grass because she is hooked on the stuff (hardy-de-har-de-har-har!), knowing very well that it will lead to the hard stuff.

Pot, too, is a steppingstone for Baker. He wants to deal in the hard stuff, like heroin and goofballs. This displeases J.R. because he is content with dealing in pot. The same cannot be said of the big boss, Mr. A (Jackie Coogan), because it nets him a meeting with the dope kingpin. The tough guy rides the dope express and gets in deeper when he turns everything upside down with a surprise twist that earns him a badge of honor.

Russ Tamblyn, as Tony Baker, speaks in the strained hipster lingo of '50s exploitation flicks and even has a passable snarl when he wields his knife. He is a spindly runt who succeeds in playing it tough because that's the way his part is written. It is amazing that he isn't wiped clean after his first encounter, stealing someone's parking space at his new school. A stiff wind could blow him over yet he asserts himself in a way that inspires terror among his peers.

He is the new kid at school, a transfer student with a horrendous scholastic record. He flashes a large bankroll, uses slang phrases and boldly lights up a joint in the principal's office. His best acting scene is when he feigns a dope high after he pretends to shoot up to impress the evil Mr. A.

Mamie plays Baker's sexed-up aunt who is continually on the prowl for her nephew. A sizzling scene is her attempted seduction of him. He is about to bite into an apple when she grabs his wrist and redirects the forbidden fruit into her mouth for a crunchy bite followed by an inviting stare.

John Drew Barrymore does not possess the thespian talent of his father, the Great Profile. Having stated the obvious, we'll take John Drew's hipster version of Columbus' arrival in the New World over pa's recitation of Hamlet's soliloquy.

The same type of praise can be heaped upon the namesake offspring of the Little Tramp. Take a single frame out of any of Papa Chaplin's talkies and you would have the equivalent of junior's acting in this film. A touch of the old man's agility exists in the son's backwards tumble after his undercover character is felled in a shootout.

One of Jackie Coogan's credits is the titular character in Chaplin's *The Kid*. Here, he is anything but youthful but fits the bill nicely as the honky-tonk piano player in the malt shop where the kids congregate to dance and listen to beat poetry. The back room is another story; it is where the underground money factory runs all night.

Jan Sterling plays Arlene Williams, the sexually repressed English teacher. She has her hands full with Baker and his aunt. Baker comes on to her during his first day in her class, asking her, "Who are you afraid of? Me or yourself?" She also gets it from Aunt Gwen when she tries to enlist the wanton woman's help in rehabilitating her nephew. It is a showdown between unbridled sexuality and sexual repression. One almost expects Jan Sterling to melt when Mamie Van Doren asks her about ever having a late date in the second balcony or taken a ride on the backseat of a motorcycle.

Diane Jurgens is sexy as the nice girl who has literally gone to pot. She appears to be squeaky clean but that is to no avail when she becomes addicted to the devil's weed. Her parents pass for the liberals for their time, attesting to their youthful boldness with tales of drinking whiskey during Prohibition.

The ubiquitous Lyle Talbot plays William Remington Kane, a crooked lawyer who works for the dope kingpin and bails Baker out of jail after he is busted for pot possession when he cracks up his hotrod during a drag race.

The legendary Vampira uses her Christian name as a student who gives an impassioned beat recital backed by Mr. A's Dixieland band. The recital is a reminder of rock 'n' roll's debt to Dixieland jazz. Jerry Lee Lewis opens the movie singing the title song on the flatbed of a truck.

Born Reckless

Born Reckless: (1958-Warner Bros.-79 min.)
Jackie Adams: Mamie Van Doren. *Kelly Cobb*: Jeff Richards. *Cool Man*: Arthur Hunnicut. *Liz:* Carol Ohmart. *Wilson:* Tommy Duggan. *Papa Gomez*: Nacho Galindo. *Mama Gomez*: Allegra Varron. *Rodeo Girl:* Jeanne Carmen. *Trailer Camp Girl*: Asa Maynor. *Rodeo Announcers:* Jack Welden and Malcolm Roselle. *Director:* Howard W. Koch. *Producer*: Aubrey Schenck. *Screenplay*: Richard H. Landau. *Story*: Richard H. Landau and Aubrey Schenck. *Cinematography*: Joseph F. Biroc. *Editor*: John F. Schreyer. *Music*: Buddy Bregman.

Born Reckless is a horse opera of a different color. The rodeo and the country music club circuits are the tracks traveled by tragedy and glamour, the central themes of the movie. Jackie Adams (Mamie Van Doren) is a trick rider and ruby-throated nightclub performer and Kelly Cobb (Jeff Richards) is an itinerant circuit rider who competes in local rodeos. Love is what keeps them together and prolongs the madness that provides fulfillment.

Kelly Cobb is a red-blooded country boy who beds his groupies and enjoys his liquor. He is coached by Cool Man (Arthur Hunnicut), a rider whose fame is a thing of the past. Cool Man relives his glory years through Cobb and they form a bond. The movie highlights the talents of the rodeo performers and provides ample display of bronco-busting and precision riding.

Mamie assumes an alluring pose as Jackie Adams in *Born Reckless*. 1959, Warner Bros. Pict. Corp.

Cool Man (Arthur Hunnicut [r]) listens while Jackie Adams softens up Kelly Cobb (Jeff Richards [l]) for the married life. 1959, Warner Bros. Pict. Corp.

    The rodeo circuit is filled with sideshow hustlers and shifty promoters just like the nightclub circuit. Jackie Adams has to face both as she is a rider and a singer. She's lucky to have Cobb and Cool Man as friends because they always bail her out of sexually compromising situations. They do this by fighting and Cobb always has his bruises ministered to by Adams in the next scene. He also has an earful of advice from Cool Man about love. Problems arise because Jackie Adams brings love into Cobb's life.

    Koch's dark style mutes *Born Restless* and makes it a seedy character study. The settings have a drab look to them and add to the sadness of the story. Adams, Cobb and Cool Man foreshadow the losers in John Huston's *The Misfits*. The trio travel the circuit and keep each other company in the twilight years of their career.

    They are on the edge of nowhere, the beginning of the nuclear age. She rides precision during the day and sings rockabilly tunes at night. Cobb is coming to the end of his riding days. Spending money as soon as he makes it has deprived him of buying the stretch of land that he wants to call home. Cool Man was once the best but now trains

Jackie Adams sings "Home Town Girl" to an appreciative crowd.
1959, Warner Bros. Pict. Corp.

his errant pupil during the last days. He is a font of bitter wisdom and realizes that Cobb's retirement would mean two has-beens instead of one.

Mamie plays Jackie Adams as a woman who has three sides to her: the nightclub singer, the trick rider and the traditional woman who wants to marry and start a family. She has a hot stage act and it agitates fans, club owners and members of the press. Adams handles them but relies on the help of Kelly Cobb and Cool Man to rescue her from the baying hound-dog men. She shows her maternal instincts when she sings "Something to Dream About," a beautiful lullaby on a Mexican ranch, inspired by the security and love of Mama and Papa Gomez's family life.

Jeff Richards' Kelly Cobb is a cord of wood who is stoic and rueful about the days to come. He rides with conviction and still has reverence for his craft but feels that his best days are over. Disappointment makes him find solace in his groupies and it begins to hasten his descent.

As Cool Man, Arthur Hunnicut still delivers what it takes to be the loyal down-home sidekick. He successfully shows the former glory and the current angst of the faded rodeo rider. Nacho Galinda and Allegra Vallon play Papa and Mama Gomez with a spiritual warmth and a happy feel to them. Carol Ohmart is a bad girl of the rodeo and Jeanne Carmen is just a plain ol' rodeo girl.

The musical score is rock 'n' roll and country-and-western music. Mamie sings "Born Reckless," "Something to Dream About," "Home Type Girl," "A Little Longer," and "Separate the Men From the Boys." Johnny Olenn and his group perform "Born Reckless" and "You Lovable You." Tex Williams sings "Song of the Rodeo," a Spanish-style ballad.

Guns, Girls and Gangsters

Guns, Girls and Gangsters: (1959-Imperial Pictures, Inc.-71m) *Vi Victor:* Mamie Van Doren. *Chuck Wheeler:* Gerald Mohr. *Mike Bennett:* Lee Van Cleef. *Joe Darren:* Grant Richards. *Ann Thomas:* Elaine Edwards. *Steve Thomas:* John Baer. *Lou Largo:* Paul Fix. *Director:* Edward L. Cahn. *Screenplay:* Robert E. Kent. *Story:* Paul Gangelin and Jerry Sackheim. *Producer:* Robert E. Kent. *Cinematography:* Kenneth Peach. *Editor:* Fred R. Feitshane, Jr. *Music:* Buddy Bregman.

Guns, Girls and Gangsters is an example of how a small out-of-the way movie can define a genre that it is a subset of. A clever heist movie that clocks in at a brief seventy-one minutes, it is a thumbnail gallery of small-time crime figures trying to set their lives straight with a grand plan. Vi Victor, Chuck Wheeler, Mike Bennett and Joe Darren form a reluctant team that undertake an ingenious plan to rob an armored car transporting Las Vegas casino money.

Vi Victor (Mamie Van Doren) is a nightclub performer drawn into the armored car robbery by chance and design. She is the estranged wife of one of the jailhouse plotters, Mike Bennett (Lee Van Cleef), and is currently the singing paramour of club owner and underworld figure Joe Darren (Grant Richards).

Victor is a point of connection for Chuck Wheeler (Gerald Mohr), a grimacing ex-con who plotted the caper with Bennett in San Quentin. Wheeler uses Vi Victor to get to Darren, whose money-laundering connections are needed to make the robbery a success.

Graphic advertisement for *Guns, Girls and Gangsters*. 1958, United Artists Corp.

Joe Darren is the common point of interest to all three characters: he is the underworld paramour of Vi Victor; Wheeler needs his contacts; and Bennett will lose control, ruin his upcoming parole by escaping, and upset the whole plan because of his lunatic jealousy.

By the movie's end, Wheeler, Bennett and Darren will have reaped the tail-end of a dead man's dreams and Vi Victor will wind up a caged canary. As she is placed in the prowl car after her arrest, the narrator

Guns, Girls and Gangsters 151

Chuck Wheeler (Gerald Mohr) coerces Vi Victor into becoming part of an armored car heist. 1958, United Artists Corp.

Grant Richards, Gerald Mohr and Mamie Van Doren iron out the details of the daring robbery. 1958, United Artists Corp.

solemnly intones that there "can be no tomorrow for those who live only for today."

The movie's closing shot is of an armored car cruising down the desert road. It is the movie's hero, a symbol of the invisible hand of free-market economics. The narrator is emphatic in telling the viewers that the armored car has a job to do and it does it well.

Mamie sizzles as the star-crossed nightclub performer. Vi Victor is a tragic and lonely figure with a soft and tender quality to her. In a scene at the roadside diner, Val waxes prosaic about the beauty of a Christmas tree's ornaments. Its freshness reminds Vi of Christmas as a child and she recalls the man who played Santa, a drunk at the mission whose only sober day was when he played the part at the department store.

She can't separate herself from the past because of the obsession of her estranged husband, the homicidal Mike Bennett. Vi Victor also struggles and sacrifices but ultimately is consumed by her ambition. She is the character left behind; the one that could have been any of the others if not for a twist of fate. Her dead-end becomes the deadly climax for the three men in her lives. They are shadows of her past, present and future. Vi is the common denominator that dooms them.

Gerald Mohr is slick and creepy as the snake oil man with the big dreams. Arrogance is a way for him to act tough and he throws his weight around with a smile that borders on a grimace. He has everything figured out until his partner's psychosis upsets the balance. Everything is askew and ends tragically for the man who had timed everything except spontaneity.

Madness and sadism are energizers for Mike Bennett. Lee Van Cleef doesn't waste any hatred in his quest for a cuckolded lover's revenge. The two-million-dollar robbery becomes secondary to the trigger-happy con who ruins his upcoming parole with a prison break.

Joe Darren has a second-tier mobster type of feel to him. His baggy eyes and cheap cigar enforce the impression. Grant Richards plays it tough in love and business until he is stunned by an unexpected death - his own. Mike Bennett facilitates a look of pain and surprise that climaxes with Darren's roadside demise.

Elaine Edwards and John Baer are the lovey-dovey owners of the gas station-motel-diner that serves as the setting of the robbery and final shootout. They are the heart that Vi Victor hides beneath her tough exterior.

Guns, Girls and Gangsters 153

Vi Victor serenades the guests at a New Year's Eve party. 1958, United Artists Corp.

The Highway Patrol arrest Vi Victor for conduct unbecoming a lady.
1958, United Artists Corp.

Mamie Van Doren sings two songs. "Anything Your Heart Desires" is a Latin-flavored nightclub production number performed at the beginning of the movie. "Meet Me Half Way, Baby" is a steamy performance at a roadside diner during a New Year's Eve party.

The Beat Generation

The Beat Generation: ('59-MGM-101m) aka This Rebel Age (USA reissue title)
Sgt. Dave Culloran: Steve Cochran. *Georgia Altera:* Mamie Van Doren. *Stan Hess:* Ray Danton.
Francee Culloran: Fay Spain. *Jake Baron:* Jackie Coogan. *Art Jester:* Jim Mitchum. *Louis Armstrong:* Himself. *Cameos:* Vampira, Maxie Rosenbloom, Charles Chaplin, Jr., Sid Melton, Grabowski, Dick Contino, Ray Anthony. *Director:* Charles Haas. *Producer:* Albert J. Zugsmith. *Screenplay:* Richard Matheson and Lewis Meltzer. *Cinematography:* Walter Csatle. *Editor:* Ben Lewis. *Songwriters:* Louis Armstrong, Albert Glasser, Walter Kent, Louis Meltzer and Tom Walston.

In *The Beat Generation*, each character has a twin that either brings blessings or curses, creating a cast of split personalities and double identities that are transfigured through redemption and resurrection principles.

A Vice Squad detective, Dave Culloran (Steve Cochran), is the principled law-and-order twin of Stan Hess (Ray Danton), a midnight rambler masquerading as a nihilistic beatnik. Culloran is a brooding granite man who is suspicious of women's motives because of an unfaithful first wife. Hess is the Aspirin Kid, a gloved rapist who leaves aspirin tins at the crime scenes.

Culloran's wife, Francee (Fay Spain), is a beatified Phoenix rising from the ashes of Puritan hypocrisy after Hess attacks her and she conceives a child by an unknown father. By refusing to take a blood test, the

Lobby poster for *The Beat Generation*. 1959, Loew's Inc.

Sgt. Culloran (Steve Cochran) harasses Georgia Altera to get a lead on a rapist. 1959, Loew's Inc.

ambiguity gives her the power to assert her independence from the granite man and his dark shadow.

Steve Cochran plays a convincing woman-hater who cloaks his feelings in statutes and alibis. His level-headed partner, Jake Baron (Jackie Coogan), challenges his impulses but is brushed off. It takes Georgia Altera's meltdown to make him face his inward shame.

Ray Danton's demented beatnik is a study in terror. He is smooth and sharp, like a knife that cuts both ways. His cowardice is exposed in the end after an underwater fight scene between him and Culloran.

Fay Spain plays a character who covers more ground, emotionally and physically, than all of the other characters combined. She is ostracized by her husband after her ordeal. It takes her independent attitude toward her pregnancy to jolt her husband from another angle.

Mamie Van Doren's character is a fearless provocateur with a brutally honest appraisal of sexual predator. Altera's strength and confidence is the source of a healthy attitude that enables her to conquer the cop and the rapist with her logic and strong-willed resistance to their sicknesses.

Georgia Altera grounds the other characters. Her attitude and style

158 The Films of Mamie Van Doren

Georgia Altera's cool and calm manner heats up Steve Cochran, Jackie Coogan and Ray Anthony (l - r). 1959, Loew's Inc.

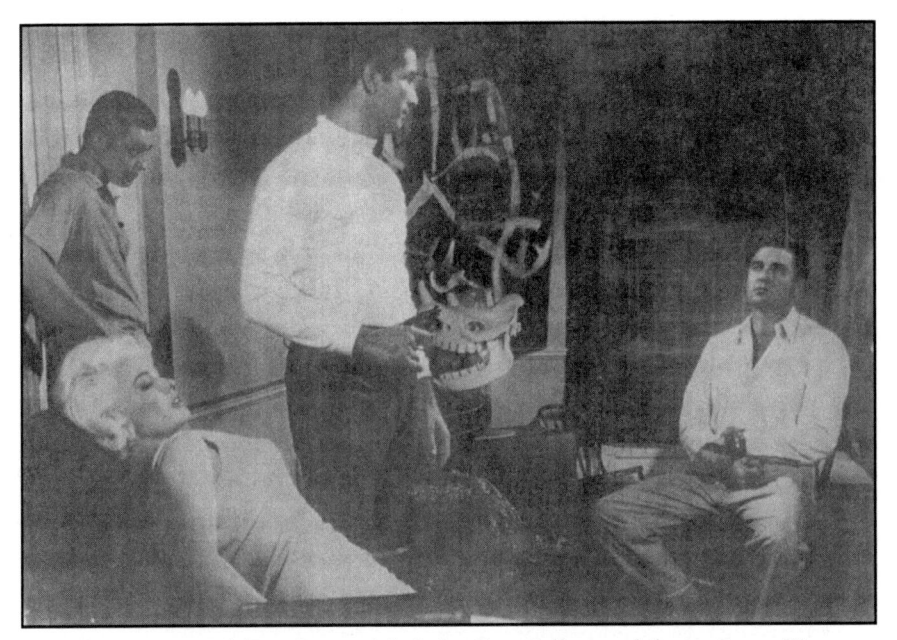

The Aspirin Kid (Ray Danton) belittles Sgt. Culloran while Art Jester (Jim Mitchum) and Georgia Altera observe him. 1959, Loew's Inc.

are the missing spokes of the wheel that connects Sgt. Culloran, Stan Hess and Francee Culloran. Her mature honesty is wrapped in a comical attitude that is strong enough to intimidate the cop and the rapist.

Equal protection under the law becomes a case of terror for Georgia Altera.

Disaffected by her separation from her husband, she is a freewheeling spirit who finds that her independence suits her. Her freedom is

The Aspirin Kid (Ray Danton) kidnaps Georgia Altera. 1959, Loew's Inc.

threatened when she becomes a pawn in an ugly game of chess between a macho cop and a rapist called the Aspirin Kid.

The Aspirin Kid uses his sidekick to initiate a series of copycat crimes to confuse the police. Georgia Altera is his first intended victim. The tables are turned when she tries to seduce him and she becomes a lure for the detective to trap the rapist. Toward the end of the film, she is kidnapped by the Aspirin Kid and the cop is taken prisoner, too.

While at the mercy of the Aspirin Kid, Georgia Altera makes pointed observations about the misogyny of the cop and the rapist. She keeps her wits and that is how she survives the ordeal. Eventually, there is a showdown between the cop and the mad man. The cop wins but not without having his own woman-hating impulses revealed.

The movie has stakeouts and shootouts, plus musical numbers from Louis Armstrong and the beat poets. Phony rock 'n' roll mixes with genuine New Orleans jazz to create a bizarre soundtrack. Included are a poetry reading by Vampira and a beat number by Ray Danton and his disciples. Zugsmith's motley cast also includes Ray Anthony, Maxie Rosenbloom, Dick Contino, Irish McCalla, Vampira, Charles Chaplin, Jr., Sid Melton and Grabowski.

The Big Operator

The Big Operator: (1959-MGM-91m.)
aka Anatomy of the Syndicate (USA reissue title)
Little Joe Braun: Mickey Rooney. *Bill Gibson:* Steve Cochran. *Mary Gibson:* Mamie Van Doren. *Fred McAfee:* Mel Torme. *Oscar Wetzel:* Ray Danton. *Tony Gibson:* Jay North. *Cliff Helden:* Jim Backus. *Director:* Charles Haas. *Screenplay:* Allen Rifkin and Robert Smith. *Short Story:* Paul Gallico. *Producer:* Albert J. Zugsmith. *Cinematography:* Walter H. Castle. *Editor:* Ben Lewis. *Music:* Van Alexander.

The televised 1951 Kefauver Hearings on labor corruption riveted the nation. Television was coming into its own as more households had sets and this contributed to the popularity of the Senate hearings. Testimonies about the Mafia's vise grip on labor unions piqued audience interest and it did not take long for Hollywood to exploit this phenomenon. *On The Waterfront* ('54) is the most popular movie dealing with corrupt labor unions.

Albert Zugsmith was never at a loss for cashing in on fads and seedy developments in American morale and his contribution to the corrupt labor union genre is *Slaughter on 10th Avenue*, starring Richard Egan, Julie Adams, Walter Matthau and Dan Duryea. He was still at it in 1959 when he produced *The Big Operator* for MGM. It is a grim and violent movie starring Steve Cochran, Mamie Van Doren and Jay North as the atypical All-American family terrorized by organized crime goon squads.

A press book cover for *The Big Operator*. 1959, Loew's Inc.

The Big Operator 163

Bill (Steve Cochran) and Mary Gibson (Mamie Van Doren) are the ideal suburban couple at the height of the Nuclear Age. 1959, Loew's Inc.

The city's blue-collar dream reached new heights in '50s suburbia. The nightmare of big city corruption followed it there with the unions. Joe Braun (Mickey Rooney) is a labor leader who wheels and deals to wield absolute control. He is the subject of a Senate sub-committee investigation. A sore point is his alleged connection to an enforcer, Oscar Wetzel (Ray Danton), known as The Executioner. Braun denies knowing Wetzel, but the prosecutor accuses him of committing perjury.

The only person who can contradict Braun is Steve Gibson (Steve Cochran), machinist at the tool and dye plant. He saw Braun and Wetzel outside the union hall the night of a meeting. It was a chance encounter and tentative, but Braun takes no chances.

His first course of action is to bribe Gibson and his pal, next-door neighbor Fred McAfee (Mel Torme.) This fails so a more persuasive course of action is employed. Oscar Wetzel and his arm twisters (Leo Gordon and Grabowski) start a reign of terror on Gibson and his family, plus the neighbors next door. The men are the main targets, but the wives are traumatized and the Gibson child is kidnapped on Halloween by Wetzel and the goon squad.

Little Joe's attempts to change Gibson's testimony only serve to incriminate himself. The final showdown is inventive if implausible as Gibson leads his posse to the house of detention

The Big Operator was one of the last brutal crime dramas Mickey Rooney made during a phase that started in the late '40s. It had a harder edge than his other pulp potboilers, only because of the Zugsmith touch.

Bill Gibson (Steve Cochran) rescues an immolated Fred (Mel Torme) while Mamie comforts Ziva Rodann. 1959, Loew's Inc.

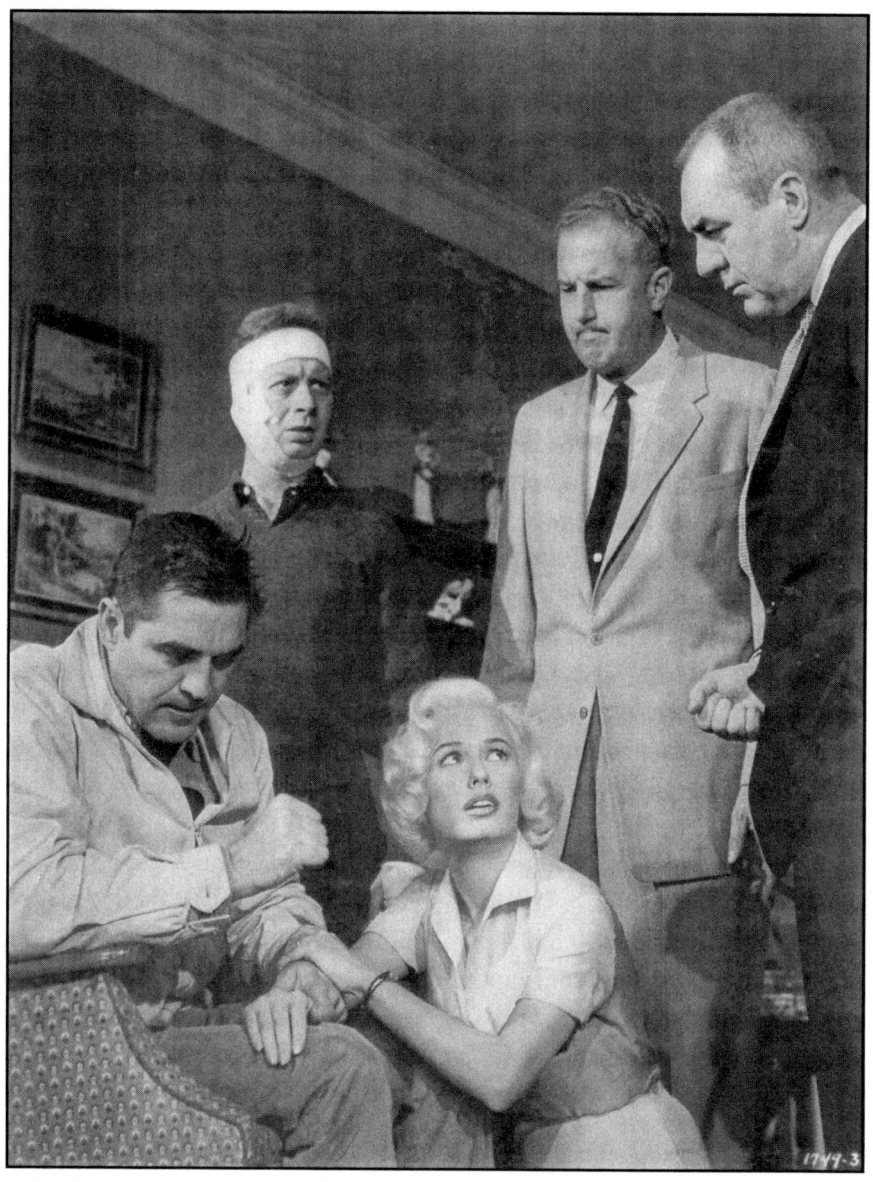

The gang tries to convince Bill (Steve Cochran) to testify against Little Joe Braun. 1959, Loew's Inc.

Rooney is kinetic and threatening as the labor boss, a livewire that fizzles because of an honest union man. He may be short in stature, but is driven by his Napoleonic complex. He bosses around everyone is sight and humiliates men twice his size. The only people he can't control are Bill Gibson and Fred McAfee.

Bill Gibson (Steve Cochran) is the blue-collar neighbor and husband of the year. He is doing his best at the tool and dye factory to give his family the best life that he can. An incidental sighting before a union meeting sets him in hot water with Joe Braun. Gibson becomes dog meat for Braun's enforcer, Oscar Wetzel. So does his neighbor, Fred McAfee.

Ray Danton is sharp as Oscar Wetzel. He is a smooth operator with a straightforward manner. The nature of his crimes makes the viewer believe that he is bloodless. Oscar Wetzel is a reptile with a pencil mustache. He heads a goon squad that includes Leo Gordon and Grabowski.

Mamie is Mary Gibson, the beautiful suburban wife and mom. She cooks, cleans and cares for her family. Nothing exists beyond the world of her husband, son and cheery next-door neighbors. The harassment of her husband and kidnapping of her son sets Mary Gibson into combat mode. She accompanies the posse to the kidnap house and knocks out a couple of the crooks with a whiskey bottle and her fists.

Mel Torme is the cheery Fred McAfee. It seems that he wishes that he was Bill Gibson. The next best thing is being his best friend. Torme's enthusiasm makes him annoying and one almost feels good about him earning Little Joe's enmity. Wetzel teaches McAfee the perils of playing with fire. The pesky survivor mixes it up with his attackers in the final free-for-all.

Jim Backus is a government agent; Jackie Coogan plays a Braun stooge and Ray Anthony is a wire-tap technician. Billy Daniels plays a stooge and Ziva Rodann has a small part as Fred McAfee's wife. Her big scene is screaming her lungs out when Wetzel dumps her husband's flaming body on their front lawn. Grabowski and Leo Gordon are henchmen under the command of Oscar Wetzel, the Executioner.

Girls Town

Girls Town: aka The Innocent and the Damned (USA reissue title) (1959-MGM-90m)
Silver Morgan: Mamie Van Doren. *Fred Alger:* Mel Torme. *Dick Culhane:* Ray Anthony. *Mother Veronica:* Margaret (Maggie) Hayes. *Jimmy Parlow:* Paul Anka. *Serefina Garcia:* Gigi Perreau. *Vida:* Gloria Talbott. *Director:* Charles F. Haas. *Producer:* Albert J. Zugsmith. *Screenplay:* Robert Smith. *Story:* Robert Hardy Andrews. *Cinematography:* John L. Russell. *Editor:* Leon Barsha. *Music:* Van Alexander and Paul Anka.

Rival gangs, hot rods, make-out spots and testosterone madness create a world where attempted rape seems like a joke because someone like Chip wants some action. The joke becomes societal ostracism for his failed conquest when Chip falls off a cliff and is killed. The curvaceous and independent Silver Morgan (Mamie Van Doren) is incarcerated because she is charged in the wrongful death of the teenage boy. Silver tries to prove her innocence while maintaining her sovereignty inside the Catholic Reformatory.

Inside, she fights a war on two fronts: the nuns who teach her discipline and a clique that tries to cure her rebellious tendencies. Silver is tough and her resilience is viewed as rebellion by a clique within the reformatory. Vida (Gloria Talbott) is a tough-fisted hen ready to devour Silver with her ju-jitsu come-ons.

Mother Veronica (Margaret Hayes) keeps a cool vigil with her passionate concern; she won't allow it to go beyond a flip and a tumble. She

Salacious German press book cover for *Girls Town*. 1960, Film Neues Programm.

is about to burst into flames because of repressed desire. Internal satisfaction is the spark given off by the brutal fights between Silver and the clique.

Silver's strength comes from the devotion of Serefina (Gigi Perreau), another inmate and pop-singing sensation Paul Anka. In the chapel, his rendition of "Ave Maria" is the salve for Silver's troubled soul. She finds an answer in a prayer to St. Jude, the patron saint of hopeless causes.

An intrepid detective (Ray Anthony) hired by the dead boy's parents digs for the facts and believes that Silver was the not the girl who was identified by Fred Alger (Mel Torme).

Albert Zugsmith previewed *Girls Town* for Cardinal Spellman. It was the setting of the Catholic institution that required the producer to show the film to the powerful cardinal, who insisted that a shower scene be excised. It showed Mamie, shoulders-up, showering and singing a Paul Anka song. It was considered too steamy for the ardent critic and the musical number was removed.

Silver Morgan is Mamie's best character. She is tenacious and cynical because she and her kid sister come from a broken home. It is familial

Silver Morgan shows off her legs when she arrives at the Catholic reformatory for wayward girls. 1959, Loew's Inc.

obligation that makes Morgan an accomplice in her own frame. Mistaken identity and a lying witness inflame the prejudice against her. Compromise is time served at a Catholic home for wayward girls.

Her adventure starts with incarceration and ends with exoneration. Silver Morgan is curvaceous with an attitude full of sass and snarl. She drives everyone insane with her charms and she uses it to her advantage. Her style works most of the time, except behind the walls of Girls Town.

Silver Morgan arrives at Girls Town and immediately challenges a nun's authority. 1959, Loew's Inc.

Silver Morgan is introduced to the power clique (Gloria Talbot, Maggie Hayes and Gigi Perreau [l-r]). 1959, Loew's Inc.

Veda is the tidal wave that cuts Silver down to size. Mother Veronica's platitudes irritate the wounds. Silver's attitude becomes more defiant. In the end, they join forces to fight the nefarious Fred Alger. Alger's duplicity is indirectly responsible for Silver's incarceration.

Perseverance provided by St. Jude turns the tide for Morgan as she proves her innocence and clears his sister from any wrongdoing in the sordid affair. She leaves Girls Town with everyone's respect and gives pointed advice to the next hellion who has arrived with an attitude.

Elinor Donohue plays Morgan's kid sister. Only Fred Alger knows her part in the puzzle and he isn't telling anyone. A frame and a blackmail scheme is the way he intimidates the sisters. Donohue is helpless and hysterical, a total victim of Alger's control. South of the border is her next destination as a hostess. It takes the Mann Act to prove Fred Alger is a coward.

Mel Torme is sleazy as the ruthless gang leader and lying eyewitness to the crime that claims the life of his buddy. He falsifies his testimony, deliberately framing Silver because she wouldn't cross colors and be his girl. Alger wins at playing chicken with a hotrod and succeeds in control-

172   The Films of Mamie Van Doren

A provocative pose for the staid retreat. 1959, Loew's Inc.

ling women with intimidation. He is brought down south of the border by a rock in a blonde's stocking with the Mother Superior as a witness.

Gloria Talbott plays it no-nonsense and tough as Veda. She uses jujitsu to tame Silver and overcome the villains at the end. Talbott heads the gang that controls things at the halfway house. She does not get any flack or resistance from the Mother Superior.

Margaret Hayes is hallowed and resolute as the Mother Veronica. She tends to the crises around her with a bemused equilibrium. She dispenses wisdom and makes correct decisions about things in general. Hayes wields an efficient high step when it is needed most and blesses the deed with detached bonhomie.

Former child star Gigi Perreau is Serefina, Silver Morgan's shadow. She pledges her help to Silver after she is beaten up by Talbott. The shadow is slightly unbalanced, having been reprimanded for nurturing a delusional relationship with Paul Anka, a nice-guy singing idol who aids Girls Town. He sings his hit, "Lonely Boy," in the movie. His rendition of "Ava Maria" to Silver in the chapel becomes her rallying cry.

Vice Raid

Vice Raid: (1959-Imperial Pictures, Inc.-71m.)
Carol Hudson: Mamie Van Doren. *Whitey Brandon:* Richard Coogan. *Vince Malone:* Brad Dexter. *Phil Evans:* Barry Atwater. *Louise Hudson:* Carol Nugent. *Captain Brennan:* Frank Gerstle. *Ben Dunton:* Joseph Sullivan. *Eddie:* Chris Alcaide. *Director:* Edward L. Cahn. *Screenplay:* Charles Ellis. *Producer:* Robert E. Kent. *Cinematography:* Stanley Cortez. *Editor:* Grant Wytock. *Music:* Paul Sawtell and Bert Shefter.

Vice Raid is a modest film that has all of the tried-and-true crime drama ingredients: ambition on both sides of the law, a sex goddess doing terrestrial duty as blonde bait, cheap plot twists, dry narration, and jazzy brass sequences with shades of strip show bumps and grinds. It also has a low budget and an abbreviated length that help make it the silver-screen equivalent of a dime-store pulp novel.

Carol Hudson (Mamie Van Doren) is a honey-coated call girl whose walk confirms the connect-the-dots entrapment scheme of racketeer Vince Malone (Brad Dexter), a solution to the question on how to bring down Whitey Brandon (Richard Coogan), a tough and honest vice cop.

Brandon's square-jawed justice irritates Malone, the local kingpin of a crime syndicate that controls narcotics, gambling and prostitution. His plan is to entrap Brandon in an extortion setup during the vice cop's undercover operation as an amateur photographer.

Carol Hudson is the model hired to frame the vice cop for indecency in a hotel room photo session. Posing in a white bathing suit and

Mamie Van Doren plays Carol Hudson, a high class call girl used for entrapment in *Vice Raid*. 1959, United Artists Corp.

matching pumps, Hudson performs a lithe dance that entices Brandon, who plays along with her overture before making the arrest. The bust backfires when the vice cop is accused of attempting to extort money from the model.

At a hearing by Internal Affairs, Carol Hudson's story is backed up by Sgt. Dunton, Brandon's crooked partner. His corroboration of Hudson's story causes the committee to boot Brandon from the force. Ostracism and disgrace only impel Brandon to clear his name by destroying Malone's vice ring.

Vice Raid is a lean crime drama. The antagonism between Carol Hudson and Whitey Brandon gives the movie its juice. As Carol Hudson, Mamie shows her charms in enough

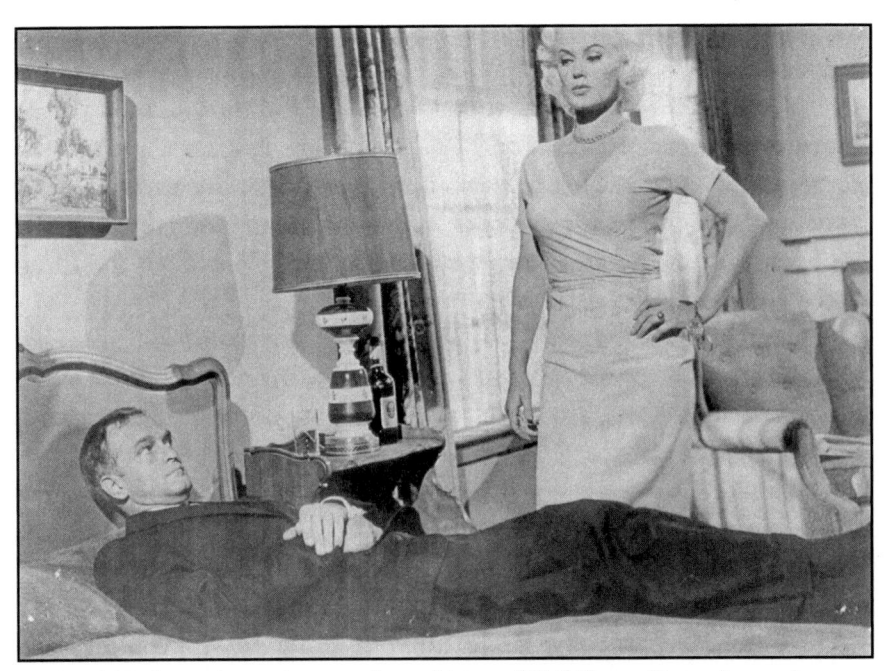

Carol Hudson tries to dampen the ambition of Phil Evans (Barry Atwater), an underling to the boss. 1959, Loew's Inc.

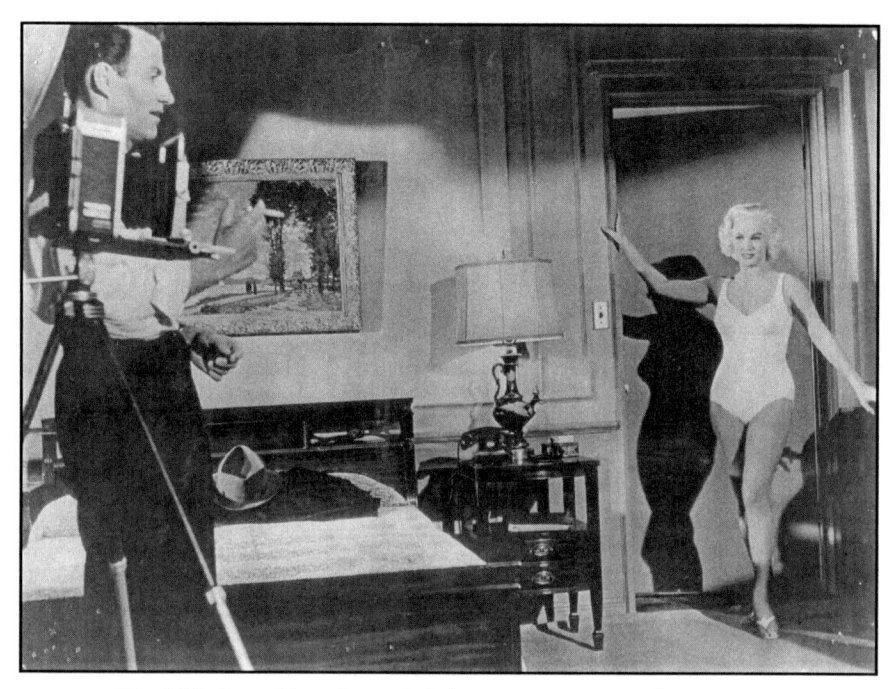

Carol Hudson shimmies and shakes to entrap an undercover cop (Richard Coogan). 1959, Loew's Inc.

ways to make her points. Examples are her fluid walk, hotel room dance and the ability to handle Brandon, Malone and ambitious underlings.

Carol Hudson is the key to busting the rackets. A savvy call girl from Michigan, she is a straight shooter whose rules of the game are survival and exclusive rights to the spoils. She plays the role of the spoiler well, acting as a strict temptress who teases and destroys while remaining exclusive property of the boss.

Hudson is controlled by Vince Malone the moment she arrives and is commanded to demonstrate her walk. It is her audition and it wins the admiration of the gangster, along with the unwanted desire of his cohort, Phil Evans (Barry Atwater). She is a brick wall that gives Whitey Brandon and Phil Evans headaches. Hudson is loyal to Malone until Evans assaults her visiting kid sister with impunity. It is then that she aids her former nemesis, Whitey Brandon.

Richard Coogan's Whitey Brandon has a straightforward attitude with angular features that make him look like the comic strip detective Dick Tracy. He is tough, honest and tenacious. He batters his opponents and survives beatings, too.

Whitey Brandon (Richard Coogan) wants to slug Carol Hudson for framing him but her younger sister (Carol Nugent) intercedes. 1959, Loew's Inc.

Joseph Sullivan as Dunton, his crooked partner, has the face of a cream puff and the body of a cheap suit hanging on a rack. He is a cop on the take; that much is for certain when the movie begins with a vice bust gone bad.

He and Whitey Brandon bust Maxie the transporter at the bus station with a Dallas model whose only credential is a photo in a girly magazine. Brandon believes in chivalry so he escorts the model back to the ticket window for a ride back home.

Dunton tells Maxie to make a break for it and shoots him dead when he runs. After he helps to frame Brandon in the entrapment case, he is ordered by Malone to kill his ex-partner. Instead, he is machine-gunned by Eddie (Chris Alcaide), Malone's muscle.

Brad Dexter plays Vince Malone as a tough guy whose eloquent hand gestures add a touch of grace to his commands. Whether it is demanding a woman who has it up here in the head, telling Carol Hudson is walk across the room and away from him or pointing to the wall safe, Dexter softens his harshness with the gesticulations.

It is all a moot point after his empire crumbles. He was once a smooth operator with dealings in gambling, numbers and dope. His lat-

Whitey Brandon (Richard Coogan) gets a leg up on crime. 1959, Loew's Inc.

est racket—a string of modeling agencies that are fronts for an escort service—invite ruin when Whitey Brandon decides to crack the rackets wide open. All of Malone's juice and power couldn't buy Brandon.

Barry Atwater plays Phil Evans, Malone's right-hand man. He is cheap and ambitious, a wannabe crime boss who upsets the balance of power because of his lust for Carol. He thinks that she will be his moll because the syndicate bosses will replace Malone with him. They prefer Brandon, whose inroads into their profits impel them to give him a cut of the total take before they are busted in a wiretap sting.

Carol Nugent plays Carol Hudson's dopey kid sister. Her yen to be a model becomes Phil's revenge scheme. It ends with Whitey Brandon seeing Carol and her kid sister board a bus back home.

Sex Kittens Go To College

Sex Kittens Go to College: aka Teacher versus Sexpot and The Beauty and the Robot (1960-Allied Artists-94 min.) *Dr. Mathilda West*: Mamie Van Doren. *Jody*: Tuesday Weld. *Suzanne*: Mijanou Bardot. *Boomie*: Mickey Shaughnessy. *Dr. Zorch*: Louis Nye. *Dr. Myrtle Carter*: Pamela Mason. *George Barton*: Martin Milner. *Conway Twitty*: Himself. *Wildcat MacPherson*: Jackie Coogan. *Prof. Watts*: John Carradine. *Etta Toodie*: Vampira. *Legs Raffertino*: Allan Drake. *Grabowski*: Himself. *Prof. Towers*: Irwin Berke. *Bartender*: Jody Fair. *Director:* Albert Zugsmith. *Screenplay*: Robert Hill. *Story*: Albert Zugsmith.

It is fitting that *Sex Kittens Go to College* was made at the dawn of the Sixties. It is Albert J. Zugsmith's eclectic vision of America as it entered the Space Age: a post-rock 'n' roll culture morphing into retro-Americana with R-rated strippers entertaining a giant robot. The moral of the story is that the human sex drive will override the computer chip given the right stimulus. In this movie, Mamie Van Doren is the right stimulus.

She plays Prof. Mathilda West, a genius who has been selected by Thinko, the campus robot, in its calculations for the right educator to bring Collins College into the Space Age. The new professor has an I.Q. of 298, 40 points above genius. She has thirteen degrees and speaks eighteen languages. Her vital statistics are 40-20-32.

Guaranteed by the computer to be the ideal choice does not sway the faculty of the college because they are threatened by her sexuality.

Besides being a genius, she is stunningly beautiful, with an earthy sensuality that awakens the repressed instincts of the other characters with the exception of the French exchange student who is conducting a research project on sex.

That is what *Sex Kittens Go to College* is, a research project on sex during an era when the Middle Ages was being challenged by Jet Set living. It is burlesque mixed with cybernetics and male-dominated moral

Tuesday Weld, Mijanou Bardot and Mamie Van Doren star in *Sex Kittens Go To College*. 1959, Loew's Inc.

Thinko the Robot oversees the burgeoning love affair between George Barton (Martin Milner) and Prof. West. 1959, Loew's Inc.

codes. The infallibility of Thinko's computational prowess is undermined by the libido of his nuts-and-bolts makeup. The philosophy of the public relations shill is that the status quo must prevail even if it means a Renaissance has to be sublimated into silent obeisance and domestic repetition. The remedy to both problems is the singular Prof. West yet she has to sacrifice her heart and soul in the end to satisfy a desire to keep up appearances for the sake of keeping them up.

Prof. West leads a Conga line that includes Voltaire the Chimp, Jackie Coogan, Irwin Berke, John Carradine and Louis Nye [l - r]). 1959, Loew's Inc.

Prof. West is an innovative scientific genius who rocks with a ballistics demonstration and a mating dance at the Passion Pit. She also short-circuits the college humanoid computer. Not even five strippers can outmaneuver Mamie. She is a natural and totally void of self-consciousness yet it is the misconception and narrow-mindedness of others that defines her. In the end, she snaps under pressure and becomes an obedient android figurine in the nuclear family's dream manual.

Martin Milner plays the love-struck public relations shill of the college. He believes that Prof. West does not fit the appropriate image of someone who heads a science department. In the end, he wins the hand of the downscaled genius.

During the metamorphosis, his nearsighted vision creates a buildup that neutralizes Prof. West's power. A curious side effect is that all of the professor's female rivals are now aggressive blondes. They do it without genius, depending solely on the blonde mystique and the power of bitchiness.

Pamela Mason does all that she can to humiliate and discredit West. Tuesday Weld's naiveté leads her to believe that the professor has amorous

Martin Milner, Louis Nye and Mamie Van Doren elude gangsters trying to collect a gambling debt from Thinko the Robot. 1959, Loew's Inc.

Mickey Shaughnessy aims his tommy-gun to keep the usual suspects in line. 1959, Loew's Inc.

intention for her boyfriend Woo Woo (Grabowski), the football captain. The only character who does not feel threatened by Prof. West is Suzanne (Bijanou Bardot), who is oblivious to anything except her sex study. She is surprisingly frank about her sexuality, but no one questions or accuses her because she is French.

Mickey Shaughnessy and Allan Drake are slapstick gangsters. Louie Nye is the science professor who programs Thinko the computer. Vampira plays the professor's spectacled lab assistant. Jackie Coogan is a rich Texas oil man doing a third-rate impersonation of W.C. Fields. John Carradine and Irwin Berke are two middle-aged erudite professors who poorly disguise struggling hormone adjustments with intellectual bravado. Voltaire the Chimp is the honorary beatnik who plays bongos and writes a book in his spare time.

Albert Zugsmith took the film beyond the teen satire genre into the realm of sexploitation when he added a scene of topless striptease performances. In a dream sequence, five strippers attempt to restore confidence to Thinko.

The Private Lives of Adam and Eve

The Private Lives of Adam and Eve: (1961-Universal-International-87 min.)
Nick Lewis/The Devil: Mickey Rooney. *Evie Simms/Eve:* Mamie Van Doren. *Lil Lewis/Lilith:* Fay Spain. *Hal Sanders:* Mel Torme. *Ad Simms/Adam:* Martin Milner. *Vangie Harper:* Tuesday Weld. *Doc Bayles:* Cecil Kellaway. *Pinkie Parker:* Paul Anka. *Passiona:* Ziva Rodann. *Devil's Familiars:* Theona Bryant, Toni Covington, Phillipa Fallon, Barbara Walden and June Wilkinson. *Satan's Sinners:* Stella Garcia, Donna Lynn, Nancy Root, Andrea Smith and Sharon Wiley. *Directors:* Albert Zugsmith and Mickey Rooney. *Writers:* Robert Hill and George Kennett (story.) *Producer:* Red Doff. *Cinematography:* Philip H. Lathrop. *Music:* Van Alexander.

The Private Lives of Adam and Eve is a black-and-white disaster movie and a tinted Creation myth rolled into one courtesy of Albert J. Zugsmith. The movie bills itself as a pipe dream, a fantasy and a fable. It involves a bewildered husband, a wife seeking a divorce, a teenage runaway, a guitar-playing boy wonder, a seedy traveling salesman, an amoral gambler, his soon-to-be-divorced wife and the kindly bus driver.

The magic bus to Reno is the point of departure for a busload of passengers with soap opera histories. Evie (Mamie Van Doren) is a wife in flight, having tired of the drab life of a mechanic's spouse. She feels the heat of Texas oilman Nick Lewis (Mickey Rooney), whose duty of the moment is to divorce his wife, Lil (Fay Spain). The other passengers are

The cover of Todo, a Mexican magazine, with Mamie Van Doren as the mother of creation. 1961, Todo.

teenage runaway Vangie (Tuesday Weld) and Hal Sanders, a seedy lingerie salesman (Mel Torme). A last-minute passenger is Pinkie Parker (Paul Anka), a teen sensation; Cecil Callaway plays Doc Boyles, the kindly bus driver.

Ad (Martin Milner), Evie's husband, is the hero of the moment when he hears a radio broadcast of an impending flood that will wash out the bridge. Using the teen sensation's defective hot rod, he races the bus, which has been commandeered by a demented Mickey Rooney. Ad becomes a passenger on the bus the hard way when his hotrod careens off the country road and over a cliff.

The flood occurs and they find refuge in a hilltop church. It is here that Doc Boyles calms the passengers and challenges the sarcasm of Nick Lewis who, in his terror, ridicules God. Ad and Evie fall asleep in each other's arms and have a tinted dream about the Creation myth where they play Adam and Eve.

Tinted stock footage of exploding comets, erupting volcanoes and natural disasters herald the birth of a new world. John Carradine intones passages from Genesis to give the process a holy connotation. Burlesque is the order of the day for the Creation myth. From sensual interludes to five-and-dime jokes, the atmosphere is low-brow all the way. Mickey Rooney plies his comic talents as the Devil. His temptresses are played by June Wilkinson and a bevy of pinup queens.

Ad (Martin Milner) and Evie (Mamie Van Doren) are about to experience the Creation myth via the dream portal. 1960, Universal Pictures Company, Inc.

There are three styles in one film: the black-and-white soap opera disaster, the colorized burlesque cosmology and a domestic comedy. It's a

Satan (Mickey Rooney) pays a house call to Eve. 1960, Universal Pictures Company, Inc.

Adam (Martin Milner) is terrified by Eve's challenge to taste the apple. 1960, Universal Pictures Company, Inc.

Adam (Martin Milner) literally falls from grace as Eve ponders her rise to power. 1960, Universal Pictures Company, Inc.

shame that the premise of the flood could not have been padded to create a full-fledged disaster epic. The prospect of seeing the principals' fight for survival would have made more interesting viewing than a series of soft-burlesque skits dealing with paradise, temptation, and domesticity.

Mamie is the movie's showcase. Her beauty was monitored by representatives of the Hays Office. No exposed navel or curves of Venus were the mandates and her blonde mane had to be glued to strategically-placed strips of rubber to avoid a wardrobe malfunction. Despite the guided censorship, the film failed to get the stamp of approval from the Legion of Decency.

Mamie's tour-de-force is her breakdown at the end of the film. It is an erotic confession of a divine dilemma. Her apology and plea for forgiveness is accepted in the form of an alternate birth to the old rib.

The most strained performance is Martin Milner's. He is annoying as the first man and comes off as being oafish. His pantomime about the birth of man is out of a third-grade acting class. The country bumpkin bit as the waif seduced by the devil's temptresses also gets on the nerves.

The part was supposed to have been played by Mickey Hargitay, but his wife, Jayne Mansfield, refused to let him star in a movie with Mamie Van Doren.

Fay Spain is alluring as the dark temptress who challenges Eve's supremacy on the links. She has her quota of tease scenes and makes the most out of the censors' boundaries. Lilith is the dark counterpoint to Eve and has to surrender her charms in order for the story to have a happy ending. But not before she has seduced Adam and made Eve the first female cuckold. It ends with Lilith's humiliation at the hands of Eve, whose victory is expulsion as she flees the garden for the second time.

Mickey Rooney is equal parts burlesque M.C. and clown. He throws out his lines with spit and polish, playing the part with a cocky attitude. The devil enjoys his manipulative relationship with Eve and cons her as an interior decorator, a makeup artist and a fashion designer who changes her image with his subtle logic. His temptresses are the cheesecake beauties of the time, including Ziva Rodann as Passiona.

College Confidential

College Confidential: (1960-Universal-International-91 min.)
Steve Macinter: Steve Allen. *Betty Duquesne. Walter Winchell:* Himself. *Henry Addison:* George Marshall. *Sally Blake:* Mamie Van Doren. *Sam Grover:* Mickey Shaughnessy. *Fay Grover:* Cathy Crosby. *Marvin:* Conway Twitty. *Edna Blake:* Pamela Mason. *Ted Black:* Elisha Cook, Jr. *Gogo Lazlo:* Ziva Rodann. *Deputy Sheriff:* Rocky Marciano. *Celebrity Columnists:* Sheilah Graham, Earl Wilson and Louis Sobol.

Professor Steve Macinter (Steve Allen) is conducting a study of teenagers' perceptions and attitudes. His research includes co-ed parties and surveys that cover a variety of perspectives. The subject that proves the most controversial is sex. The project is sanctioned by the college and even given an apologia by the old fart dean (Herbert Marshall). That doesn't stop an irate father (Elisha Cook, Jr.) from challenging the decency of the study after his daughter (Mamie Van Doren) claims that the professor kept her out until three in the morning as a part of his survey.

Pretty soon, the town is up in arms because of the study and the *Times* dispatches a female reporter (Jayne Meadows) to chronicle the story. She is sympathetic until he shows a porno movie at one of his parties with the college students. The hysteria becomes a witch hunt and the professor is put on trial, which becomes public when famed journalists and columnists arrive to cover it. Titillation takes a backseat to questions about sexuality and the definitions of beauty as the nation monitors the trial of the smut professor.

Mamie Van Doren plays Sally Blake, a confused college student whose lies lead to a smear campaign against a progressive professor. 1960, Universal Pictures Company, Inc.

The trial is the highlight of the movie. It takes place in the general store because the shop owner is the magistrate, among other municipal titles. He is played by Mickey Shaughnessy, who always delivers when called upon to give an impassioned performance. Shaughnessy exudes small-town cornpone, welcoming a contingent of celebrity journalists, which includes Walter Winchell, Earl Wilson, and Louis Sobol.

A small town becomes the media eye and homespun wisdom degenerates into the warped ambition of a hayseed jurist. Many angles, from the cheap to the unusual, are used to forward the story and it has something for everyone bent on a prurient kick.

The movie is a comedy by today's standards. The musical numbers are rock 'n' roll spoofs and the sordid issues are now the subject of conversation on a.m. gabfests. It is the unusual combination of actors and celebrities, plus tawdry plot twists, which gives the movie its points of interest.

Steve Allen plays an egghead who wants to quantify the moral rot that is slowly corroding esthetics of beauty in America. He comes off as slightly seedy because of his intrusiveness. It's not just the Kinsey-like questionnaire; that is optional. He films the kids at the grotto where they have their polite hootenannies. The rock 'n' roll was limp and it was the dawn of the beach party phenomena. The professor is the curious oldster, a character that would become a staple in the beach party movies.

Jayne Meadows is the reporter sent to sort things out for the Times. She observes in an aloof manner until the party where the professor is framed.

Newspaper reporter, Betty Duquesne (Jayne Meadows), watches as Prof. Macinter (Steve Allen) is busted on a morals charge. 1960, Universal Pictures Company, Inc.

Sally Blake is sworn in at Prof. Macinter's hearing by the judge-grocer played by Mickey Shaughnessy. 1960, Universal Pictures Company, Inc.

She is outraged that the punchbowl was spiked and the home movies of the hootenanny turned out to be porno. The reporter does a complete 180-degree turn and even passes on the story when the trial is over. She has found her First Amendment knight and it is the start of something big.

Mickey Shaughnessy could play it straight or strictly for laughs. In *College Confidential*, he gets to mix styles. Shaughnessy is a small-town

Clarence Darrow as he argues and decides the law. An enterprising man, he also runs a small grocery store. His dark side comes out when he is revealed as the man who framed the professor. He unravels as he explains his reasons to the courtroom crowd, lost in a daze that embarrasses his daughter and everyone who knows him.

Mamie is surprisingly staid as Sally Blake, as if June Cleaver were playing a rebellious high-school teenager. Her dark deed is that she lied about the professor to cover up a late date with Conway Twitty. She does not have much to do outside of having a loud argument with her parents and act innocent as a witness at the trial.

Pamela Mason and Elisha Cook, Jr. get top honors of weird couple of the year. She acts as if she were doing a nervous breakdown scene from a weepy romance and he still delivers a macabre performance mainly because he was typecast with menace by the time he made this movie.

Walter Winchell, his career given a brief resurgence because of his narration of *The Untouchables*, leads the pack of famous journalists who cover the trial. Only the great Winchell has lines, as he narrates the trial in his inimitable clipped style. Stunt casting includes Rocky Marciano, the former heavyweight champ, and famous columnists like Sheilah Graham, Earl Wilson and Louis Sobol playing themselves.

The Blonde From Buenos Aires

The Blonde From Buenos Aires: *original title: Americana en Buenos Aires, Una (Argentina)* (1961-D'an-Fran-80 min.)
Stars: Mamie Van Doren, Jean-Pierre Aumont, Carlos Estrada, Catherine Zabo and Chela Ruiz. *Director:* George Cahan.

Every star has an obscure film that is so rare that it seems invisible. This is Mamie's hard-to-find film.

Cover of Radiofilm, a magazine that chronicled Mamie's trip to Argentina to film the movie. 1961, Radiofilm.

The Candidate

The Candidate: (1964-Atlantic Releasing Corp. -84 min.) aka Party Girls for the Candidate aka The Playmates and the Candidate
Samantha Ashley: Mamie Van Doren. *Angela Wallace*: June Wilkinson. *Frank Carlton*: Ted Knight. *Buddy Barker*: Eric Mason. *Mona Archer*: Rachel Romen. *Dr. Endicott*: Herb Vigran. *Party Girls*: Carol Ann Lee, Joyce Nizzari, Beverly St. Lawrence, Susan Kelly, Sharon Rogers and Suzanne Hiatt. *Director:* Robert Angus. *Producer*: Maurice Duke. *Screenplay*: Joyce Ann Miller and Quentin Vale. *Music*: Steve Karmen. *Cinematography*: Stanley Cortez. *Editing*: William Martin.

Buddy Barker (Eric Mason) is the subject of a Senate Committee investigation trying to prove that he built his empire on the judicious use of sex and vice. The charges include corrupting a Senate candidate and two women. In his quest to build an empire, Buddy Barker builds a ladder out of the people he uses then burns it when he reaches the top and finds out that he's bottomed out. It happens after a wild party, the kind where someone gets left holding the bag.

The chief witness against him is Samantha Ashley (Mamie Van Doren), his number one manipulator. She is the sunshine blonde of the Eisenhower era who didn't know when to leave the party. Samantha is the chess piece that thinks for herself and can make her own moves. It is her recruitment of the prize manipulator that sets things in motion for the downfall of everyone involved.

Angela Wallace (June Wilkinson) is a stunning statuesque beauty who is initiated into Barker's inner circle of party girls by Samantha Ashley. Her mark is Frank Carlton (Ted Knight), the blonde-haired and square-jawed Senate candidate from Massachusetts. They actually fall in love and plan to marry.

Pressbook cover for *The Candidate*, a film that would seem topical today. 1964, Cosnat Productions.

Frank Carlton (Ted Knight), a candidate for the Senate, is surrounded by his loyal supporters. 1964, Cosnat Productions.

Barker vetoes this by showing Carlton an old stag reel of Angela's cinematic virtues, hoping that the candidate will change his mind about her. Barker gets more than he bargained for when Carlton dies from a heart attack because of the shock. Repercussions result with the collapse of Barker's empire and the dissolution of his power by virtue of Senate proclamation.

Van Doren paints Samantha Ashley with soft shades and sharp lines. The character would be considered a soap opera heroine today, but in 1964 Ashley was a fallen woman about to be shown the back door. An unacknowledged player, she becomes a mover and shaker with her testimony.

Eric Mason was touted as the next new something and his role as Buddy Barker was supposed to be living proof of it. The only noteworthy thing about the role that it is a fake profile of Bobby Baker, disgraced stalwart in Lyndon Johnson's circle. Notoriety was Mason's key to press and his performance is an asterisk in political scandal movies. His ill-fated puppet is the one slated for success and recognition.

Ted Knight plays the straight-as-an arrow Senate candidate. A supporting player in '50s television, this was his first big role. Ten years later, he would gain a place in television archives as Ted Baxter, part of the ensemble that backed Mary Tyler Moore in her self-titled show. The popularity of the Baxter role led to his own show, *Too Close for Comfort*.

The legendary and enigmatic June Wilkinson plays Angela Wallace, the irresistible lure that bends the political schemata and exposes the statesman as a partisan pimp. In the end, all the dirt rubs off on him and Wilkinson becomes as American as apple pie because she once made a man's heart skip a beat.

Herb Vigran, a gruff character actor known to many Fifties' television crime drama buffs, has a moribund part as an abortion doctor who loses control and molests his patient. The disturbing scene is the basis of a cover up that is uncovered and displayed on trial when it is revealed that the woman was there courtesy of Barker. It was all because of the wild party.

Stanley Cortez is the cinematographer of *The Candidate* and he infuses the movie with the soft focus style of *The Magnificent Ambersons*. Cortez filmed mostly second-string productions after the Orson Welles classic. By the Sixties, his best was *Shock Corridor* and *The Naked Kiss*, two films directed by Sam Fuller. On the other end of the scale was a

Buddy Barker (Eric Mason) explains the machinations of Washington politics to Samantha Ashley. 1964, Cosnat Productions.

Twisting the night away at a wild Washington party. 1964, Cosnat Productions.

movie like *They Saved Hitler's Brain*. Regardless of the film, it still had the royal look of his best years.

The Candidate is considered a sordid gimmick picture because its topicality was taken from the headlines. It also pushed the boundaries of censorship with two versions. The plot of *The Candidate* seems contemporary, but in 1964 it was considered lurid and taboo. To consider the dark underpinnings of politics would have been laughable and subversive. Public service undermined by sexual hi-jinks, drunken debauchery and backstreet abortions was not something the American movie audience felt comfortable with. Washington was rocked by the Bobby Baker scandal, but that was considered an exception to the norm.

It is another Mamie Van Doren movie that may seem like a drawing room comedy by today's standards but upset the public morals squads back then. It was deemed another example of how cinema was degenerating into cheap tricks in order to compete with the ascendancy of television. Big screen productions pushed the envelope with daring themes so it was natural that exploitation films did the same. The irony is what was exploitation in '64—sexual misconduct in the nation's capital with the resultant sordid retribution—is now topical.

The era's strict societal mores were reflected in the handling of the release of *The Candidate*. Some movie magazines jokingly called it the first foreign movie made in the United States because the overseas version included nudity. The title was also changed to *The Candidate and the Party Girls*.

Three Nuts In Search of a Bolt

Three Nuts in Search of a Bolt: aka 3 Nuts and a Bolt (USA) (1964-Harlequin International Pictures -78 min.-B&W/C)
Saxie Symbol: Mamie Van Doren. *Tommy Nooman*: Himself. *Dr. Myra Von*: Ziva Rodann. *Joe Lynch*: Paul Gilbert. *Bruce Bernard*: John Cronin. *Dr. Otis Salverson*: Peter Howard (Howard Koch). *Director*: Tommy Noonan. *Screenplay*: Tommy Noonan and Ian McGlashan.

Saxie Symbol (Mamie Van Doren) is a stripper who hates men. Her neurosis is a censured libido. Joe Lynch (Paul Gilbert) is a salesman and bitter alcoholic. He drinks all day and that includes having cereal with whiskey instead of milk. Bruce Bernard (John Cronin) is a narcissistic model who distrusts women. The prettiest face that he's ever seen lives in the mirror and he wishes that he could get access to it but he can't. The three neurotics recognize their need for counseling but cannot afford to see an analyst of note.

They decide to get the best psychiatric evaluation available for one third the rate by hiring Tommy Noonan, a Method actor, to impersonate their phobias. It is Noonan's task to listen to their problems and assume their symptoms so he can relate them to a famous psychiatrist, Dr. Myra Von (Ziva Rodann). He would relay the advice and solutions to his benefactors.

Trouble ensues because Noonan gives their problems equal time and this gives the analyst the impression that he has three personalities: the man hater, the woman hater and the people hater. This intrigues the

A suggestive herald for *3 Nuts in Search of a Bolt*. 1964, Harlequin Int. Pict.

Mamie Van Doren strikes a sensuous pose as the demented stripper, Saxie Symbol. 1964, Harlequin Int. Pict.

doctor and she hooks up a closed-circuit television to hold a conference with other noted doctors. The wires are crossed and the private session is broadcast nationwide. The show is a hit and the principals are the subjects of exploitation by producers and hustlers. Ethics problems follow and are resolved in the most plaintive way: through money and delusion.

The premise of *3 Nuts in Search of a Bolt* is a blueprint for a great screwball comedy. Tommy Noonan's vision was bigger than his accomplishment. The result is an oddity that has its charm and merits but also possesses many nuisances and contrivances. Hilarity turns into weirdness many times in this movie because the characters are edgy and borderline psychos. Today, the movie would make a topnotch reality show.

The movie has many funny parts, mainly due to Tommy Noonan's hilarious impersonations of his co-stars. He plays the Method actor who relates the trio's problems and mimics their voices and movements with on-the-mark impersonations, especially when he does Saxy Symbol. Zivann Rodann plays Dr. Myra Von, the psychiatrist who blows the whole thing out of proportion.

Joe Lynch (Paul Gilbert) is so grotesque that his vitriol is hilarious. He is a spitfire comic earning a living as a used car salesman. Alcohol is what fuels his fury and he is a hot iron ready to press anyone into steamed submission.

Mamie Van Doren pushed the buttons for the censors with her steamy beer bath. 1964, Harlequin Int. Pict.

Joe Lynch (Paul Gilbert) is a hopeless alcoholic who amuses Saxie Symbol and Tom Noonan. 1964, Harlequin Int. Pict.

Mamie Van Doren drives a television executive wild with her programming ideas. 1964, Harlequin Int. Pict.

Bruce Bernard (John Cronin) is a bitter pretty boy model from the South. His moment of corruption came as a child when he was held after class and molested by a spinster. Hardly the stuff of laughs the movie makes it out to be, it is one of the movie's frequent detours into weirdness.

Mamie has a field day as Saxy Symbol, the stripper pushed over the edge by sexual role playing. Her performance is sensual and bizarre, a multi-faceted personality that includes icy, kittenish, determined and neurotic. In one scene, she shares a dark secret with Noonan and regresses into a thumb-sucking infant. It is another example of how the laughs turn into nervous silence.

Last, but certainly not least, are the teasers of the movie - two color sequences that feature Mamie in a beer bath and a striptease. They were the movie's selling points, along with a six-page pictorial in *Playboy*. Noonan had an earlier success with the same set-up in *Promises, Promises*, starring Jayne Mansfield. She, too, spiked the movie with an eight-page layout in *Playboy* magazine.

The soap suds of the beer bath was a foamy toast to the Legion of Decency and Mamie's striptease is a grand example of a lost art. She upholds the tradition of burlesque exotica with a fluid style that shows the modern world what tassels were all about.

3 Nuts in Search of a Bolt was banned in New York until legal issues were settled.

The Sheriff Was a Lady

The Sheriff Was a Lady: aka Freddy im wilden Westen (West Germany); In the Wild West; The Wild, Wild West (USA) (1964-Avala Film-101 min.-C)
Black Bill/John Burns/Freddy: Freedy Quinn. *Olivia*: Mamie Van Doren. *Steve Perkins*: Rik Battaglia. *Anita*: Beba Loncar. *Joana:* Trude Herr. *Sheriff:* Carlo Croccolo. *Harry*: Klaus Dahlen. *Murdock*: Vladimir Medar. *3 Bandits*: Stole Arandjelovic, Milivoje Popovic-Mavid, and Mirko Boman. *Ted*: Josef Albrecht. *Director*: Sobey Martin. *Screenplay*: Gustav Kampendonk.

Freddy Quinn was considered West Germany's Elvis Presley. Just as Presley had *Love Me Tender,* Freddy Quinn had *The Sheriff Was a Lady*. Quinn plays Black Bill, a singing Teutonic cowboy who plays the guitar and is fast on the draw. He often breaks into a song, whether on the prairie trail, a boom town saloon, at the gravesite of a friend or the film's final quest. Black Bill's trademark is tossing a silver dollar into the air and shooting a hole through it. He also has a demented laugh that echoes across the plains. Justice is the ace he keeps up his sleeve and it is a card trick that keeps him alive.

Black Bill rides to avenge the ten-year-old murder of his parents. Added to his quest are finding Ted Daniels, a recently kidnapped rancher, and honoring the memory of his young daughter, both victims of an attack on their ranch. The cowboy's sense of justice is most striking of all of his character traits. He is the lone gunman who braves odds that outnumber him by a sizeable margin when he goes up against Perkins, a land baron, and the town that he owns.

The German press book cover for *The Sheriff Was a Lady*. 1964, Obel Film.

Perkins owns the bank, the hotel, the saloon and everything else in Moon Valley. His autocratic rule is threatened by the arrival of Black Bill, who travels under the name of Burns. He is a wise guy who fans the flame of Olivia (Mamie Van Doren), the singer at the Last Chance Saloon. This is Perkins headquarters and Olivia belongs to him. The upset of the balance of attraction causes friction between Burns and Perkins.

The underlying cause of the tension is the kidnapped miner, who is held captive in the saloon's basement. He is being sweated for info about his gold mine and the map that he hid in his gold watch. His daughter (Beba Loncar) has survived the ranch massacre and arrives in Moon Valley, looking for her pa.

The matron at the sheriff's office advises her to change her name and talks her into becoming the deputy sheriff. His boss is the sheriff - the town drunkard. She conducts her own investigation, comes to odds with Burns, whom she thinks is the culprit, and unwittingly abets Perkins in his takeover until a reversal of fortune at the film's end.

Freddy Quinn is a nerdy hero whose success is based on the lameness of his opponents. He can sing and shoot a hole through a silver dollar. Acting sincere in a maudlin way is another one of his feats. The clean-cut character of western hero is treating his women like angels and having a righteous contempt for evildoers.

Beba Loncar is the lady sheriff and she plays her part with courage and conviction. Loncar is tough and relentless in bringing order to the chaotic frontier town. She does this by making an overt error, which is to assume that Freddy is the bandit responsible for her father's kidnapping.

It is this misunderstanding that makes the hero work harder to solve the dilemma with a little help from the saloon goddess, who tells him

Freddy Quinn serenades Mamie Van Doren and Beba Loncar as the new sheriff in town. 1964, Obel Film.

Mamie Van Doren plays Olivia, the bawdy dance hall queen who goes from kept woman to town liberator because of love. 1964, Obel Film.

about the town boss's secrets. Her betrayal earns her freedom as she watches the hero make his ride into the prairie landscape.

Mamie's betrayal is the heroic move of the story. Her life is linked to the saloon owner; without him, she is nothing. She is seduced by the hero's sense of honor. Her valor is a substitute for satisfied passion. She sacrifices everything for him and winds up with nothing in the end. She stands by a tree in a field and watches the hero lead a caravan out of the villa while the former sheriff, his childhood friend watches from the comfort of home. It is the lady sheriff who gets the hero because they have a common link: they were once close childhood friends.

The Las Vegas Hillbillys

The Las Vegas Hillbillys: aka Country Music, USA (USA video title) (1966-Woolner Bros.-90 min.-C)
Woody: Ferlin Husky. *Boots Malone*: Mamie Van Doren. *Tawny*: Jayne Mansfield. *Jeepers*: Don Bowman. *Donald*: Robert V. Barron. *Henchman*: Richard Kiel. *With*: Bill and Christian Anderson, Wilma Burgess, Roy Drusky, Sonny James, Duke of Paducah, Del Reeves and Connie Smith. *Director*: Arthur C. Pierce. *Screenplay*: Larry Jackson.

The Beverly Hillbillies reinvigorated the bucolic trend in the mid-'60s. They were more pleasant than the Ma and Pa Kettle because the Clampetts were more personable. Low-budget Hollywood producers picked up on television trends and country-western movies hit the regional drive-in circuit.

One of the themes was using country-western concert footage and adding staged scenes to give it a narrative. An early example is *Second Fiddle to a Steel Guitar*. Arnold Stang is a country music lover whose musical tastes clash with his opera-loving wife. Leo Gorcey and Huntz Hall parody their famous Bowery Boys roles as stagehands at the opera house.

The Las Vegas Hillbillys is one of these exploitation films and not afraid to capitalize on the Clampett family. Legal threats forced the intentional misspelling in the title, but the connection was already made. The added attraction was having Mamie Van Doren and Jayne Mansfield star in the movie. Unfortunately, it was '66 and not '56 and the names of the Woolnor Brothers meant the drive-in circuit and not a spotlight premiere.

220   The Films of Mamie Van Doren

DVD cover for *Las Vegas Hillbillys*. 2001, VCI Home Video.

The times had changed and it was if glamour queens never existed. In this movie, they are unlikely guardian angels to a goodhearted simpleton who has inherited a broken-down casino. They provide him with the spirit he needs to make it a success.

The Last Vegas Hillbillys   221

Boots Malone charms Ferlin Hersky with a risqué dance.
1966, Woolner Bros. Pictures, Inc.

Woodrow Wilson Weatherby (Ferlin Husky) hauls wood and is trying to distance himself from his cousins' moonshine racket. He delivers the wood for their still but refuses to haul the shine. The bigger picture is hitting it big in show business. He believes it is in the stars when he inherits a Las Vegas casino from his uncle, the success of the family.

Aunt Clem gives her nephew and his buddy, Jeepers (Dow Bowman), her blessings and his fiancée tries to understand his move to catch a dream in Las Vegas. He does not understand it either when he finds out that the casino is a roadside dive that is $38,000 in debt.

Boots Malone (Mamie Van Doren) is the hostess that fills Woody in on things.

Jayne Mansfield gives it all that she's got in a musical highlight from the movie. 1966, Woolner Bros. Pictures, Inc.

Ferlin Husky and Boots Malone are blown away by the bikers who invade the club and put on a musical number. 1966, Woolner Bros. Pictures, Inc.

Her contract comes with the place and she is the indentured hostess until the end of the year. Her duties include singing and dancing, along with serving beer to the customers. She has the power to control the bikers who ride their choppers through the bar and even remains standing after the bikers turn into a country hoedown version of "Dixie." Boots is the spirit of the sawdust and stale beer bluegrass specials.

It is Aunt Clem who sees the big picture when she hires Tawny (Jayne Mansfield), an old singing protégée of the deceased uncle. She is larger than life and turns the red ink into black gold when she packs the casino with her contacts, various country-western singing stars.

Ferlin Husky will please his fans with his laid-back, easygoing country manner.

Husky sings a bunch of songs and has a daydream that will also please fans of the genre. Country-western stars perform songs as a wish fulfillment to making the Golden Circle Casino a success. Fantasy performers include Bill Anderson, Wilma Burgess, Roy Drusky, Sonny James, Duke of Paducah, Del Reeves and Connie Smith.

Don Bowman plays Jeepers, a best buddy who is the ambitious dreamer that pushes Woody out of the backwoods and into the limelight. Jeepers is a blend of James Dean and Leo Gorcey. He hunches his shoulders and speaks in a cool drawl, beady-eyed and smirking like a man with a plan. He also uses malapropisms to make his points and finds himself in situations that need the right routine to bail him out. There is even a hat that resembles the chief's.

Mamie plays Boots Malone, the hostess who keeps order in the casino. She is like the spirit of a haunted saloon, a leftover who translates it all for Husky. Boots is Husky's guide through the low-budget debauchery. Mamie sings "Free Out of Lovin'" and "Sweet Sweet Baby." She also welcomes an over-the-hill Jayne Mansfield to the Twilight Zone.

Jayne Mansfield is a cross between a Christmas tree and a space ship in the bizarre role of Tawny. She is statuesque and seems to be battery-operated. However, her rendition of "That Makes It," a "Chantilly Lace" sound-a-like, is priceless. Her only props are a red settee and two male chorus toys.

Louis Quinn, best known as Roscoe on *77 Sunset Strip*, is a loan shark ready to collect the uncle's debt from his nephew Woody. Richard Kiel (*Eegah!*, *The Human Duplicators* and *The Spy Who Loved Me*) plays his bodyguard and no-nonsense thumb buster.

The Navy vs. the Night Monsters

The Navy vs. the Night Monsters: aka Monsters of the Night; The Night Crawlers (1966-Standard Club of California Prod.-87 min.-C)
Nora Hall: Mamie Van Doren. *Lt. Charles Brown*: Anthony Eisley. *CPO Fred Twining*: Bill Gray. *Ens. Rutherford Chandler*: Bobby Van. *Marie*: Pamela Mason. *Dr. Arthur Beechum*: Walter Sande. *Bob Spalding*: Phillip Terry. *Diane*: Kaye Elhardt. *Director*: Michael A. Hoey. *Screenplay*: Michael A. Hoey. *Novel*: Murray Leinster. Cinematography: Stanley Cortez. Editor: George White. Music: Gordon Zahler.

The Navy vs. the Night Monsters is an example of how cheap 1960s horror films served as a popularity meter of '50s icons a decade after their salad days. Mamie Van Doren, Anthony Eisley, and Bill Gray had reaped the advantages of Fifties pop stardom. Mamie was a Universal-International starlet and a star at MGM. Eisley was one of the stars of *Hawaiian Eye*, a popular private-eye show featuring Robert Conrad, Connie Stevens and Poncie Ponce. Bill was once Billy, who played the beloved Bud of the Anderson clan in *Father Knows Best*. As the Hippie Revolution was in full blossom, Mamie, Eisley and Bud fought carnivorous vegetation on a remote Pacific atoll.

Gao Island serves as an Air Force weather station and refueling pad for planes in transit. It is noted fondly because of Nurse Nora (Mamie Van Doren) and Lt. Diane (Kaye Elhardt). The tropical atoll is about to experience the Ice Age when Operation Deep Freeze makes an emer-

226   The Films of Mamie Van Doren

Video cover for *The Navy Vs. The Night Monsters*.
1982, Paragon Video Productions.

gency landing on the runway. The goony bird needs more than refueling, such as a new crew and passenger list to replace the ones that disappeared between last contact and a crash landing without landing gear.

The audience knows that it is the killer trees spawned by the bacteria brought back from the Antarctic expedition. They consumed the airborne geologists, most of the crew and bailed out before the plane landed with the sole survivor—the shocked pilot. The plants breed in the hot springs and come out only at night. They pose more than a nuisance because their carnivorous appetite is mobile. The killer trees are reminiscent of the menaces in *Day of the Triffids* and their destruction recalls the climax of *The Crawling Eye* when napalm from headquarters saves the day.

Anthony Eisley plays it like he's still making time in Hawaii. He runs the show and claims victory in the end when the Navy beats the night monsters. Eisley still had what it took to play the dashing and forthright lead. He proves it with the fistfight with his chief rival, a kiss of assurance from his lady love and the successful battle against the man-eating trees from the Antarctic.

He is aided by Van Doren, who is grim-faced and two-fisted in this adventure. She is also prim and proper in her nurse's uniform and blonde ponytail. The nurse loves the Army man and tries to rebuff an unwanted suitor played by Phillip Terry.

Nurse Hall and the kindly Dr. Beechum (Walter Sande) tend to the wounded pilot of the downed airplane. 1966, Paramount Pictures Corp.

Nurse Hall lends a sympathetic ear to Lt. Brown (Anthony Eisley) as he confesses his love for her. 1966, Standard Club of California.

Terry plays his mad-at-the world guy and shines when he battles the killer trees in a head-on confrontation. Kay Elhardt is the nurse that provides the charm in this film. She has a close-encounter scene that sizzles and she emerges with the victors in the end. Walter Sande is likeable as the kindly professor who has answers for everything.

Bobby Van, the song-and-dance man, plays a goofball officer whose comic charm makes good fertilizer. Pamela Mason finally shook off her elitist attitude by 1967, but little good did it do her inside the deadly tendrils. Gray's acting tour-de-force is a death scene in the jungle after his arm is torn off by one of the monsters. He runs toward the camera and collapses. If only the movie was in 3-D.

You've Got To Be Smart

You've Got To Be Smart: (1967-World-Cine. Ass.-Stage 19 Prod.-88 min.-C)
Nick Sloane: Tom Stern. *Jerry Harper:* Roger Perry.. *Connie Jackson:* Gloria Castillo. *Miss Hathaway:* Mamie Van Doren. *D.A. Griggs:* Preston Foster. *Methusaleh Jones:* Jeff Bantham. *Methusaleh's Brothers:* Mike and Fritz Bantham. *Directed, Produced and Written by:* Ellis Kadison. *Music:* Stan Worth.

Nick Sloane (Tom Stern) is a canned L.A. ad man who embarks on a cross-country auto jaunt that will change his fortune. In Arkansas, he takes a wrong turn off the main road and winds up on an obscure byway called Platitude. A wily hitchhiker (Shug Fisher) promises to show Sloane the way if he gets a lift to where he is going.

The Way is a country revival meeting headed by Methusaleh Jones (Jeff Bantham), a child firebrand preacher, and his two brothers (Mike and Fritz Bantham). Their message is "him who loves ain't got time to hate." The catchy tune invigorates the townsfolk at the revival meeting.

Sloane sees the light in the form of dollar signs and convinces the children to return with him to L.A. His reasoning is that he is building a mammoth church because L.A. is a sinful city in need of being saved.

In L.A., Sloane sells the idea of a fifteen-minute spot to Jerry Harper (Roger Perry), a television executive. The spot becomes a sensation. Jones refuses to be sponsored by corporate greed and settles on contributions from the electronic congregation.

The preacher becomes disillusioned when he sees Sloane's dark side. The ad man is two-timing Connie (Gloria Castillo), his lovely assistant and nanny to the boys. The dark lady is Miss Hathaway (Mamie Van Doren). It all comes to a head when Sloane is busted by the D.A. and the I.R.S. for siphoning off the non-profit funds for his personal use.

You've Got to be Smart is a musical without pizzazz, a country movie without rural charm and a love story without passion. It is amateurish and bogged down by annoying leads and boring lapses of action. From the cardboard acting of the leads to the uninspired interaction between them, this movie is noteworthy only because it is a pit stop for Mamie Van Doren.

The child preacher and his brothers look like Huck Finn rejects from a rural version of *Village of the Damned*. They are played by the Bantham Brothers. Jeff is Methusaleh and he has the only speaking part. Mike and Fritz are dutifully sidekicks, keeping their mouths shut but offering support when needed.

Tom Stern is lackluster and it is puzzling that he could play the lead in a feature film. He is most suited to an obnoxious comic relief sidekick type. His L.A.-sin city musical number at the beginning of the film is a monologue with bad timing. His attempts at charming behavior come off as strident and overbearing.

Stern plays a character that is awkward and obnoxious yet persuasive. He is hated by his associates because he is a slimy character yet he can draw Connie Jackson away from his rival, Jerry Harper. Adding insult to ignobility, he starts an open affair with Miss Hathaway (Mamie Van Doren), the daughter of a steel magnate who sponsors some of Harper's shows.

As Connie Jackson, Gloria Castillo is the only bright light to this film even though she is wasted through lackluster direction. Her musical numbers are lumbering and bogged down in static boredom. Her first number, which is pensive and sensitive, ends with her almost being run over by a car. She is rescued by Jerry Harper, the television exec with the heart of gold.

Roger Perry, as Jerry Harper, is like an inflatable doll with glasses. He, too, is persistent but as in a catatonic Zen stupor. His perseverance pays off when the movie ends with love on the tarmac: Jerry unites with Connie as the plane with the kids takes off for Arkansas.

A trade ad for *You've Got To Be Smart*. 1967, Cine Associates.

Preston Foster, former star of the '30s, provides the only acting passion of the movie. He plays O.C. Driggs, a powerful ad man who fires Sloane because the underling stole an account from him. It is the dismissal that starts the country tour that nets Sloane his ill-gotten reward. O.C. returns at the end, full of fire and acuity as he assesses the set-up to Jerry Harper, whom he respects. O.C. encourages the love between Connie and Jerry.

Mamie has three short scenes as Miss Hathaway, the temptress. She meets Sloane for the first time and makes a pass at him and later lays claim to him in a restaurant where they are discovered by Methusaleh Jones. Her last scene is at the end, when Connie surrenders what rightfully belongs to Hathaway. She tells Sloane that her daddy will aid him in his case with the Feds.

Voyage To the Planet of Prehistoric Women

Voyage to the Planet of Prehistoric Women: aka The Gill Women; The Gill Women of Venus (1968-The Film Group-78 min.-C)
Moana: Mamie Van Doren. *Venusians*: Mary Marr, Paige Lee, Margot Hartman, Irene Orton, Pam Helton. *Astronauts*: Gennadi Vernov, Georgi Tejkh, Vladimir Yemelyanov, Yuri Sarantsev and Georgi Zhzhyonov. *Director*: Peter Bogdanovich. *Screenplay*: Henry Ney.

The trouble with films stitched together from other movies is that they rarely work. It takes a satirical slant or a clever touch of editing to unite different movies to create a coherent new one. Although cohesion is not one of the movie's strong points, it succeeds in producing a strange hybrid using the original as the subtext.

In the case of *Voyage to the Planet of Prehistoric Women*, the original film was *Planeta Blur*, a Russian quickie. In 1965, the Russian film was re-edited with footage starring Basil Rathbone and Faith Domergue. It was re-titled, *Voyage to the Prehistoric Planet*. Three years later, the footage with Rathbone and Domergue was replaced with new footage starring Mamie Van Doren as the matron of a clan of telepathic Venusians.

The Russian footage alternates between the story of four cosmonauts in orbit and shots of miniature toy space stations and rocket ships. The toy models are one of the highlights of the movie. The American retread has a voiceover by the movie's director, Peter Bogdonovich, which explains the inner angst of one of the cosmonauts. The narration is a bridge for the audience to cross in order to enjoy the trip through the

Cover for the DVD release of *Voyage to the Planet of Prehistoric Women*. 2004, Alpha Video Dist.

cosmos. The explorers land on Venus and this leads to further disruption of continuity with scenes of a telepathic aquatic Amazon tribe.

Moana (Mamie Van Doren) is their leader and she commands them via verbal thoughts. The tribe worships a pterodactyl that is killed by the cosmonauts when it attacks their craft. A highlight is the scene where the women cradle the rubber bird after it is washed ashore. Moana and her clan pay their respects to the fallen god and return it to the sea. The tribe sees it from another point of view and declares war on the invaders.

It is air versus water and the hotter magnetism is what melts the elements in the end. Moana and her clan have mental powers that shame the death ray and robot man of the cosmonaut invaders. They use their minds to melt mountains and turn rocks into molten streams that drive the earthmen's robot protector insane. It collapses into the lava flow and melts as the crew boards their craft and flees Venus.

Liberation from a life of servitude is the wisdom of leadership in a world ruled by Moana. Her clan is an all-blonde crew that comes off like lethargic '60s go-go dancers. Despite their freedom from men, they are not totally autonomous. Their god is a rubber pterodactyl. Its death by the laser ray of the invading males starts a war with the sea clan and the cosmonauts hightail it to the stars in the end.

Victory brings autonomy because the invaders are gone and the pterodactyl no longer has to be flattered. The new dichotomy is between the clan's hatred for their defeated fallen god and the mystical awe of the departed cosmonauts. In the clan's eyes, the cosmonauts are more powerful because they destroyed the pterodactyl.

Van Doren, the cosmonauts, the miniature toy space stations and the rubber pterodactyl keep the movie going because they are power symbols in a battle for supremacy. The toy space stations, mechanical land rover and stealth robot are the invaders' arsenal. The windswept surf pounding against the rocks is the power channeled by the clan women.

Moana inspects the remains of a robot vulcanized by lava. 1968, Film Group.

The Venusian Amazons anoint the remains of the earthlings' robot as their new power icon. 1968, Film Group.

The mental communiqués are the equivalent of dry narration. It is the re-interpreted dialogue that gives meaning to the movie because the cosmonaut's narration and Moana's mental directives are the texts for the battle in the Garden of Eden. One can lose patience between the narration and the telepathic messages the women send each other.

Nothing can be said about performances because there are none. The cosmonauts either man their ship or ride around in the land rover and the sea queens prance around in scenes that come off like bad home movies. The footage of Moana and her clan could have been edited into a strange short film that would give the theme more power and edge than it has in this patchwork quilt.

The Arizona Kid

The Arizona Kid: original title: I Fratelli di Arizona (Italy) (1971-Phillipines Prod.-C)
Ambo, The Arizona Kid: Chiquito. Bernard Bonning. *Coyote*: Gordon Mitchell. *Sharon Miller*: Mamie Van Doren. *Director:* Luciano Carlos. *Screenplay*: Lino Brocka and Luciano Carlos.

Chiquito is a popular comedian in the Philippines. Gordon Mitchell is a heavyweight on the Eurocine market. Mamie Van Doren is a galaxy unto herself. *The Arizona Kid* is a strange turn in each star's career; it was if they dreamed the same bad movie.

For Chiquito, it must have been a career highlight and for Gordon Mitchell, it was collecting another paycheck for a knockoff imitation in the genre that made him a popular European actor. For Mamie Van Doren, it is the best and worst of both worlds. She is radiant in her bustier, low-cut gowns and smooth flowing hairstyle, but is saddled with a weird assortment of sordid characters in a fight to survive situations that come with her wagon train migration. She also has a dubbed voice right out of cartoon land and becomes the unlikely paramour of the dusty and uncouth antihero played by the comic sensation from nowhere.

Ambo (Chiquito) arrives in 1900s San Francisco from the Phillipines so he can visit his uncle. A letter is all that is waiting for him and it instructs him to go to Mexico. He hops a stagecoach that is ambushed and robbed, stranding him in El Dorado. A language barrier and the need to fulfill the serving needs of a cantina give him a chance to earn room and board as a cook and waiter. He is inept and his

238   The Films of Mamie Van Doren

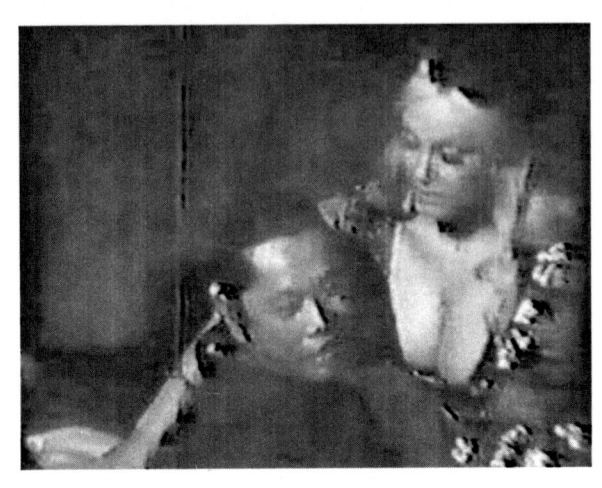

Chiquito is flummoxed as he reaches a career highlight by starring with Mamie Van Doren. 1971, Premiere Productions.

culinary specialty enrages an outlaw who drops by for a meal of soup and bread. His wrath claims the life of the kindly owner who gave Ambo the job.

The Arizona Kid, a notorious outlaw, arrives in town and kills the bandit for the hell of it. He is there to meet the niece of the slain cantina owner. It was her uncle's idea to have her hire the outlaw to kill Coyote (Gordon Mitchell), a notorious bandit who leads a gang of rampaging marauders that has been ransacking her town during harvest season.

The revenge motive is Ambo's unintentional quest as a series of mishaps derail his purpose and he winds up impersonating The Arizona Kid as a way to inspire the townspeople to return to defend their homes against Coyote. In the end, the townspeople battle the gang as Ambo has a comical duel in the sun with Coyote. He wins the duel through dumb luck and becomes a folk hero.

The hero and his lady love ride off into the sunset after he saves a town from savage marauders. Seriously! 1971, Premiere Productions.

If this sounds familiar it is because the format has been milked dry since *The Magnificent Seven,* which was inspired by Akira Kurosawa's *Seven Samurai.* Despite having a solid foundation, the movie flounders and squanders all of its inspirational elements. Bad editing, horrid dubbing, lousy continuity and full-blown performances are the causes. There is a likeable theme which, along with the score, is the second best thing in the movie—the first being Mamie Van Doren.

It is mind-boggling that Chaquito is a famous comedian in his native Philippines. He is lame and lacks timing and other essential comic skills. Three funny faces are all he has to his bag of tricks. He speaks shrill Filipino throughout the movie and it only makes his performance more irritating.

His routines range from language misunderstandings to clumsy slapstick attempts to carry out a task. He is a reluctant gunslinger, someone who has to be coaxed into it by Sharon Miller's seductions. His funniest bit is screwing up his face and crossing his eyes when he presses his cheek against Van Doren's bountiful cleavage.

Mamie plays Sharon Miller, who enters the mess stranded in a Conestoga wagon, singlehandedly warding off a band of attacking Indians. Miller is rescued by Ambo and the couple who have taken him along on the trip to their villa. She is the temptress who breaks down Ando's ambivalence and puts the pep in his step.

Her magnetism is marred by an annoying dubbed voice. If the pitch was any higher, it would shatter eardrums and drive dogs insane. She is beautiful and alluring, so it is truly disgusting to see her make out with the repulsive Chaquito. She even rides off with him in the end when they share a single saddle out of town.

Despite Mamie's travails, she still fares better than Gordon Mitchell. His performance consists of snarls, growls and scowls. Once a rugged leading man of popular Eurocines, he looks embalmed.

Free Ride

Free Ride: (1986-Galaxy-82 min.-C)
Dan Garten: Gary Hershberger. *Greg:* Reed Rudy. *Jill Monroe*: Dawn Schneider. *Carl*: Peter DeLuise. *Elmer*: Brian MacGregor. *Dean Stockwell*: Warren Berlinger. *Nurse Debbie Stockwell*: Mamie Van Doren. *Kathy*: Bebette Props. *Edgar Ness*: Chick Vennera. *Vinnie Garbagio*: Anthony Charnota. *Director:* Tom Trbovich. *Producers*: Tom Boutross and Bassem Abdallah. *Screenplay*: Ronald Z. Wang, Lee Fulkerson and Robert Bell. *Story*: Ronald Z. Wang. *Cinematography*: Paul Lohmann. *Editor:* Ron Honthaner. *Music*:

Dan Garten (Gary Hershberger) is a brash college student who tries to impress a woman at a disco by borrowing a flashy car and taking it for a joyride. He does not realize that the car he passes off as his own has a quarter of a million dollars in mob money stashed beneath the front seat. The chase begins when the mobsters appropriate a cab and follow their car to The Monroe School, a boarding school for well-heeled boys. So begins the old cat-and-mouse game, '80s style; that means that it is crude and sophomoric.

All of the stock characters are present at The Monroe School: the two hotshot buddies against the world, the nerd who desperately tries to fit in, the muscle-bound dimwit, the women who vie for nativity queen, the inept authority figures who double as the undermined oldsters, the ethnic comic relief and the hot-to-trot school nurse.

Greg Novak (Reed Rudy) is the other half of the cool duo, who patterns their styles after Paul Newman and Robert Redford in *The Sting*.

The cover for the video release of *Free Ride*.
1986, Galaxy International Entertainment.

They make the usual vows about eternal brotherhood and evade the gangsters, humiliate the Herculean oaf, educate the nerd in worldly matters, spy on women taking showers in the finishing school and devise the plan that destroys the mobsters.

The watered-down godfather is Old Man Garbagio (Frank Campenella). Campenella is a veteran actor with an impressive resume and he peppers his character with wit and threat. Vinnie, Vito and Murray are the family variants on *"Veni, Vidi, Vici."* There is no sense of the Corleone filial obligation among the sons. They use a chainsaw to sever pop's arm as retribution for stealing their money and hiding it in the hijacked car. He is given a prosthetic arm for his birthday and it has more handy gadgets than a Swiss Army knife.

Debbie Stockwell is the school nurse and she is a wonder to behold because she is played by Mamie Van Doren. It is 1987 and Mamie is playing a stock sexpot role in a college romp movie. This is twenty-seven years after *College Confidential!* What was hinted at in the professor's questions in 1960 was now on display for all to see for a vicarious thrill.

Nurse Stratton is the school's perpetually horny Florence Nightingale. She plays her scenes for tease and laughs and mixes slapstick with heated intentions. It is impressive to see how Mamie holds her own with the younger actresses who have nothing on her. She heats things up without taking anything off.

Mamie's best scene is her physical exam of the students in the gym. She wears a stylized nurse's outfit, has Playtex gloves and grooves to the beat of her song, "Young Dudes," as she grabs the students' nuts and asks them to cough. "Young Dudes" is part of the movie's soundtrack.

Nurse Stockwell has her hands full. 1986, Galaxy International Entertainment.

The Glory Years

The Glory Years: (1987-TVM-HBO-1987-140 min-C) *John Moss*: George Dzundza. *Gerald Arkin*: Archie Hahn. *Jack Sanders*: Tim Thomerson. Tawny Kitaen. *Sydney Rosen*: Joey Bishop. *Norma*: Donna Pescow. *Drummond*: Chazz Palminteri. *Director*: Arthur Allan Seidelman. *Producer*: Gary H. Miller. *Screenplay*: Gary H. Miller. *Cinematography*: Stan Taylor. *Editor:* Janet Ashikaga. *Music*: Rocky Davis and Dave Fisher.

Teen-angst and mid-life hopelessness have been given due treatment in their respective domains over the years. Every generation of moviegoers gets to experience an adolescent coming-of-age movie cycle. The '50s rock 'n' roll rebel, the '60s militant non-conformist, the '70s hard-edged kung fu disco king, and the amoral '80s cyber-punk are some of the molds that make up the genre.

The same thing can be said about mid-life reevaluation of values crisis movies. The '50s labeled the breakdown as going soft; the '60s proclaimed the change as rebirth through a new vision; and the '70s whitewashed the victims with labels of sensitive and caring. The '80s was the only decade where mid-life insecurities resulted in sophomoric hijacks and libido resurrection schemes.

The conceits of the Baby Boomers facing their Ward Cleaver moments created a return to teenage histrionics. Such an unlikely symbiosis was already legitimized when '50s macho attitudes reinvented itself as '70s disco baroque. It was the narcissistic Eighties that combined the coming-of-age genre with the mid-life crisis soap opera in juvenile com-

The cover for the video release of *Glory Years*.
1987, HBO-Mogul Communications.

edies that starred middle-aged adults.

The Glory Years is a mid-life escapade triggered by memories that are revived at a twentieth high-school reunion. Three pals from the old days meet at the reunion and the devil-may-care sparks are rekindled as middle-age blandness gives way to high rolling in Las Vegas. The only problem is their kitty belongs to the Alumni Committee and they need a way to replace it once they lose it at gambling in all the wrong places. They try to recoup their losses with various schemes and that adds more trouble to their woes.

John Moss (George Dzundza), Gerald Arkin (Archie Hahn) and Jack Sanders (Tim Thomerson) are the drunken lout, insecure second-guesser and the suave brains. They fall back into adolescent mode from the moment they hook up at the high-school reunion. Tawny Kitean is the sex kitten who jilted her original fiancé at the altar. She loves Saunders and helps him escape his negative paybacks. Donna Pescow is a lonely waitress who falls in love with Stone. Donna Denton plays Gina, the hooker with the golden heart who restores the flagstaff in Gerald's softness.

Mamie Van Doren has a small part as a Sin City brothel madam in *Glory Years*. 1987, HBO-Mogul Communications.

Joey Bishop is the father of Kitean's jilted groom, a men hellbent on revenge because the marriage would have meant the merger of two garment district families. Mamie plays Minnie, a smooth and sophisticated bordello madam who helps Sanders set up his buddy Arkin for a resurrection.

The focal point of the movie is Sanders, who is portrayed as a creep with style by Thomerson. A happy ending prevents everything from souring by having Tim and Tawny marry, Moss and Norma next in line and Gerald returning to his estranged wife.

The Glory Years is an HBO presentation and pretty tame by cable standards. At best, it is a minor addition to Tim Thomerson's career credits, although it gives Archie Hahn a chance to break away from commercials and bit parts to showcase his talent.

The Vegas Connection

The Vegas Connection: (1999-TVM-C)
Matt Chance: Robert Carradine. *Gina:* Kathy Shower. *Al Ross:* Ed McMahon. *Rita:* Mamie Van Doren. *Tom Smothers:* Himself. *Director:* Lou Vadino. *Screenplay and Executive Producer:* Dennis Lanning. *Producers:* Suzanne De Laurentis and Serge Poupis. *Cinematography:* Dwight F. Lay.

Hawaii was the favorite exotic spot for private-eye or cop shows over the years. It wasn't until *Miami Vice* became an interloper in the mid-'80s that the trendy locale was Miami. Las Vegas always lurked as a feasible third. Neon, gambling, call girls and murder still rang a bell with the public.

In the '90s, Hawaii and Miami ran their courses and Las Vegas claimed a resurgence in popularity. Neon and tackiness replaced sunsets and oceans. *The Vegas Connection* is one of the many made-for-television movies that capitalized on sin city.

Robert Carradine is Matt Chance, retired F.B.I. Agent-turned-hotel security and fashion photographer. Kathy Shower plays his girlfriend Gina and Charlie, his former F.B.I. partner and ex-girlfriend, is played by Ashley Brooks.

A rhino with snake tattoos make for Gabriel the villain, played by Ryan "Rhino" Michaels. Ed McMahon is Ed Ross, the casino boss. The Smothers Brothers are the comic relief. Mamie plays Rita, the owner of a topless dancers club.

They star in a sharp and glitzy movie about diamond smuggling, beautiful high-rollers and neon-lit murders. The movie was a pilot for a prospective television series.

250   The Films of Mamie Van Doren

Mamie Van Doren around the time she appeared in *The Vegas Connection*. 1997, Julie Strain/Femme Fatales Magazine.

Slackers

Slackers: (2002- Alliance Atlantis International Pictures- 1 hr. 27 min.-C) aka Les Complices (Canada: French Title)
Dave Goodman: Devon Sawa. *Sam Schechter*: Jason Segal. *Jeff Davis*: Michael C. Maronna. *Angela Patton*: James King. *Reanna*: Laura Prepon. Mrs. Patton: Leigh-Taylor Young. *Mrs. Van der Graaf*: Mamie Van Doren. *Director*: Dewey Nicks. *Producer*: Neal H. Moritz *Screenplay*: David H. Steinberg. *Cinematography*: *Editor:* Tara Timpone. *Music Supervisor*: Amanda Scheer-Demme.

The college frat movie craze continued into the 21st Century with movies like *Slackers*. In this movie, students are conniving backstabbers and muckrakers, a reflection of the glorification of greed in American society. Slick upwardly mobile preppie types are involved in a cheating scandal and the subsequent blackmail scheme pulled off to cover it up. Along the way, there are the sexcapades and befuddled old-timers, this time around free to vent their spleens unabashed.

This time around, the incredibly cool trio is Dave (Devon Sawa), Sam (Jason Segal) and Jeff (Michael C. Maronna) and they are about to graduate college even though they have never taken an honest exam. Their specialty is stealing the exams and copying the answers. Bomb threats, staged fires and other stunts are their modus operandi. It all comes to an end when Ethan (Jason Schwartzman), a jealous nerd, uncovers their scheme and threatens to have them expelled unless they agree to his blackmail terms.

The cover for the video release of *Slackers*. 2002, Pyamide Productions.

It seems that he is obsessed with Angela (James King), a willowy blonde who does not know that he exists. It is understandable because he is not likeable in any way because he is a deranged stalker type. His obsession includes an altar of trophies that includes photos, panties and a doll made out of his dreamboat's hair. There is not one iota of personality that can endear him to the audience. It is a relief when the tables are turned on him and he is branded a cheater.

Mrs. Van der Graf (Mamie Van Doren) demonstrates her oral technique to Jason Schwartzman, a volunteer hospital worker. 2002, Pyamide Productions.

He forces the cool trio to accept his terms: fix him up with Angela or face expulsion. What follows is a frantic adventure where the cool ones gather as much information on their mark in an effort to educate the nerd so he can appeal to her. It backfires when Dave falls in love with her and screws up the works, upsetting everyone, including Angela, who becomes aware of the original scheme.

A strange symbiosis in the youth-oriented risqué comedy trend is the appearance of former genre stars in small parts. In this movie, Leigh-Taylor Young and Mamie Van Doren have the cameo honors. Leigh Taylor-Young was the fresh-as-a-daisy flower child in hippy-themed movies like *I Love You, Alice B. Toklas!* ('68), *The Big Bounce* ('69) and *The Buttercup Chain* ('70). Here, she is a well-to-do middle-aged stepmother of one of the female marks and likes to go down on the kids, so to speak. Van Doren, bedridden in the hospital, plays a former street lady who worked the docks in her salad days. Both women get to display a sample of their oral techniques; only one of them shows why the bullet bra was made for her. Where have all the flowers gone? To *Slackers* and beyond.

Appendix I: Television

The Lux Video Theatre: Witness for the Prosecution. (9.17.53-CBS)
A.J. Mayheme: Edward G. Robinson. *Romaine Vole/ Mrs. Mozson*: Andrea King. *Leonard Vole*: Tom Drake. *Intermission Guest*: Mamie Van Doren. *Director*: Richard Goode. *Writer*: Anne Howard Bailey.

A Star Is Born Premiere: Herself. (1954)

What's My Line? : Episode #355. (3.24.57-CBS)
Guest Panelist: Melvyn Douglas. *Mystery Guest*: Mamie Van Doren. *Contestant*: Thomas Eagleton.

The Bob Cummings Show: Bob Meets Mamie Van Doren.(2.03.59-NBC)
Guest Stars: Mamie Van Doren and Rose Marie. *Director*: Bob Cummings. *Writers*: Paul Henning and Dick Wesson.

Alcoa Theatre: Girls About Town.(11.02.59-NBC)
Maybelle Perkins: Mamie Van Doren. *Charlotte Dunning*: Virginia Field. *Lacey Sinclair*: Gale Robbins. .

The Comedy Spot: Meet the Girls. (8.30.60)
Maybelle "The Shape" Perkins: Mamie Van Doren. *Charlotte "The Brain" Dunning*: Virginia Field. *Lacey "The Face" Sinclair*: Gale Robbins.

The Jack Benny Show: Death Row Sketch.(2.12.61-CBS)
Guests: Mamie Van Doren, Gerald Mohr and Alan Dexter.

The Dick Powell Show: No Strings Attached. (4.24.62-NBC)
Dick Powell. *Judy Maxwell*: Angie Dickinson. *Penny Nichols*: Mamie Van Doren. *Bunny Easter*: Barbara Nichols. ___: Leo B. Gorcey. *Danny Cannon*: Robert Strauss. *Director*: Hy Averback. *Writers*: Bob O'Brien and Ben Starr.

The Real McCoys: The Farmer and Adele. (12.30.62-CBS)
Amos McCoy: Walter Brennan. *Luke McCoy:* Richard Crenna. *George McMichael:* Andy Clyde. *Adele Webster*: Mamie Van Doren. *Michael Bowen*: Grant Richards. *Students*: Oloan Soule and James Maloney. *Director*: David Alexander. *Writers*: Ed James and Seaman Jacobs.

The Adventures of Ozzie and Harriet: Exotic House Mother. (12.09.64-ABC)
Ozzie Nelson, Harriet Nelson, David Nelson and Ricky Nelson: Themselves. *Wally:* Skip Young.

Valentine's Day: Yen Hu Horowitz. (11.13.64-NBC)
Valentine Farrow: Tony Franciosa. *Rockwell "Rocky" Sin:* Jack Soo. Libby: Janet Waldo. *Grover Cleveland Fipple:* Eddie Quillan. *Mamie Van Doren:* Herself. *Yen Ku Horowitz:* Aki Hara. *Meiko Yarawa:* Bebe Louie. *Dore Chong:* Linda Ho. *Director:* Jerry Hopper. *Writers*: Bernard Wiesen and Hal Kanter. *Executive Producer:* Hal Kanter. *Theme:* Lionel Newman. *Director of Photography:* Harold Stine, A.S.C.

Burke's Law: Who Killed 711? (12.09.64-ABC)
Pepe Van Heller: Hans Conreid. *Tristram Corporal*: Broderick Crawford. *Sam Atherton*: Dan Duryea. *Clarissa Benton*: Rhonda Fleming. *Harold Harold*: Burgess Meredith. *Aurora Knight*: Mamie Van Doren. *Cindy:* Suzzane Cramer. *Director*: Sidney Lanfield. *Writers*: Gwen Bagni and Paul Dubov.

Mr. Roberts: In Love and War. (4.01.66-NBC)
Alice Blue: Mamie Van Doren. *Lyons*: Sammy Shore. *Edmonds*: Walter Matthews. *Director*: Leslie H. Martinson. Writer: Don Tait.

The Hollywood Squares: (1.02-7.'67-NBC)
Host: Peter Marshall. *Guests*: Paul Lynde (regular), Mamie Van Doren, Noel Harrison, Barbara Feldon, Michael Callan, Abby Dalton and Morey Amsterdam

Merv Griffin: (8.03.70)

The Tonight Show: (9.02.71 & 3.05.'73)

Vegas: Serve, Volley and Kill.(12.20.'78-ABC)
Bobby Howard: Randolph Mantooth. *Katie Howard*: Pamelyn Ferdin. *Millie Farmer*: Dawn Wells. *Tommy Circo*: Red Buttons. *Sid Green*: Don DeFore. *Nicky Trent*: Christopher George. *Sandra Wells*: Lynda Day George. *Spa Manager*: Mamie Van Doren. *Director*: Sutton Rolley.

Fantasy Island: The Stripper/ The Boxer.(2.10.'79-ABC)
Billy Blake: Ben Murphy. *Jake Gordon*: Forrest Tucker. *Maureen Banning*: Larraine Stephens. *Sheba*: Mamie Van Doren. *M.V. Banning*: Stacey Keach, Sr. *Whoopee Hoover*: Chuck McCann. *Betty*: Beverly Powers. *Director*: Lawrence Dobkin. *Writers:* Ron Friedman and William Douglas Lansford.

L.A. Law: Rhyme and Punishment. (12.16.'93)

Unseen Hollywood: Herself in an interview. 1998.

Screen Tests of the Stars: Herself. 2002.

Cleavage: Herself. 2002.

Celebrity Naked Ambition: Herself. 2003

Appendix II: Theater

Billion Dollar Baby: Jackie Gleason-1951

Dames at Sea: Arlington Park Theatre

Gentlemen Prefer Blondes: Drury Lane Theatre, Chicago Wildcat

Silk Stockings (1963): Earl Wrightson and Lee Grant.

Will Success Spoil Rock Hunter?: Arlington Park Theatre

How to Succeed in Business Without Really Trying

See How They Run: Alhambra Dinner Theater-1968

In One Bed and Out the Other: Alhambra Dinner Theater-1971

A Dash of Spirits: Alhambra Dinner Theater-1976

Scandalous Follies: Reginald Gardiner, Irving Harmon, Michael Dominico, Claire Theiss.

Two and Two Make Sex

Makin' Whoopee: Imogene Coca-1980

Appendix III: Discography

SINGLES:

Salamander / Go, Go Calypso-Prep 100-(1957)

Something to Dram About / I Fell In Love-Capitol (1957)

Here's to Veterans (16" single with Ray Anthony) - The Veterans' Administration (1950s)

Nobody But You / A Lifetime of Love-Dot-15883 (1959)

Beat Generation / I'm Grateful-Dot (1959)

Bikini With No Top on Top / So What Else is New (with June Wilkinson)- Jubilee (1963)

Boy Catcher's Theme / Cabaret-Audio Fidelity (1966)

State of Turmoil (12" single): State of Turmoil (vocal)/ State of Turmoil [short version]-instrumental) -Corner Stone Records-1984

Young Dudes (12" single): Young Dudes (extended dance mix)/Young Dudes [single]/ Queen of Pleasure-Rhino-1986

Marilyn/ Edge of Hollywood (1999)-

EPs:

Untamed Youth (Rolling Stone/ Salamander/ Oo Ba La Baby/ Go, Go Calypso) (1957-Prep M 1-1)-Prep Records-1957

ALBUMS:

As In Mamie…: You and Me and Tonight/Rub It In/Quantanamera/ You Talk Too Much/ Ragtime Cowboy Joe/ Lifetime Lover/ When You're Smilin'/Alice Blue Gown/Never on Sunday/ I Wanna Be Loved. Churchill Records-

The Girl Who Invented Rock and Roll: The Girl Who Invented Rock and Roll/Something to Dream About/ Salamander/ Go Go Calypso/ Rollin' Stone/ Oo Ba La Baby/ Separate The men From The Boys/ The Beat Generation/ I'm Grateful/ Nobody But You/ Lifetime of Love. Rhino-1986.

COMPILATIONS:

Free Ride-Original Soundtrack-1985
    "Young Dudes"

Va-Va-Voom!- Screen Sirens Sing. 1985.

Beat, Beat Beatsville! -Beatnik Rock 'n' Roll-1988
    "The Beat Generation"

Rockin' Boppin' Girls-1994
    "Nobody But You"-"Rollin' Stone"

Hollywood Hi-Fi: 18 of the Most Outrageous Celebrity Recordings Ever! "Bikini With No Top on Top" with June Wilkinson.

Divas Exotica-1999
    "Go, Go Calypso."

Appendix IV : Books

The following books were used as source material for the biographical portions of the essays.

My Naughty, Naughty Life. Mamie Van Doren (as told to Richard Bernstein and Robert J. Rhodes). Century Publishing Co. 1964

I Swing. Mamie Van Doren. Novel Books, Inc. 1965.

Playing the Field. Mamie Van Doren w Art Aveilhe. G.P. Putnam and Sons. 1987.

BearManorMedia
P O Box 1129 * Duncan, OK 73534

Welcome, Foolish Mortals...
THE LIFE AND VOICES OF PAUL FREES By Ben Ohmart

The official, heavily illustrated biography of the Master of Voice. Read all about the man behind the voices of Disneyland's *Haunted Mansion*, the pirates in the *Pirates of the Caribbean* ride, Boris Badenov from *Rocky & Bullwinkle*, The Pillsbury Doughboy and thousands of radio shows including *Suspense, Escape, The Whistler* and more.

ISBN: 1-59393-0046 $29.95

Every old-time radio and cartoon fan in the world will want this book.

Foreword by June Foray. Afterword by Jay Ward biographer, Keith Scott.

"For the first time in print, the real Paul Frees is revealed. Author Ben Ohmart looks beyond the voices to uncover the man within, coming up with an evenhanded, but honest portrait of a very complicated individual. This is the definitive biography of an amazing artist."
— Laura Wagner, *Classic Images*

How Underdog Was Born
by *Buck Biggers & Chet Stover*
ISBN—0-59595-025-9
$19.95

www.bearmanormedia.com
Visa & Mastercard accepted. Add $5 postage per book.

They say there's nothing like a good book...

We think that says quite a lot!

BearManorMedia

P O Box 1129 • Duncan, OK 73534
Phone: 580-252-3547 • Fax: 814-690-1559
Book orders over $99 always receive FREE US SHIPPING!
Visit our webpage at www.bearmanormedia.com
for more great deals!